Knepper

Devil on the Deck

Devil on the Deck

Lois Hoadley Dick

Fleming H. Revell Company
Old Tappan, New Jersey

Scripture quotations in this volume are based on the King James Version of the Bible.

Library of Congress Cataloging in Publication Data

Dick, Lois Hoadley.
  Devil on the deck.

  Summary: A fictionalized account of the early life of John
Newton, who spent many years as a British merchant seaman
and ship captain before retiring from the sea to become an ordained minister, hymn writer, and outspoken opponent of the
slave trade.

  1. Newton, John, 1725–1807—Juvenile fiction.
[1. Newton, John, 1725–1807—Fiction. 2. Seafaring life—
Fiction. 3. Christian life—Fiction. 4. Slave trade—
Fiction] I. Title.
PZ7.D5466De 1984   [Fic]   83-9479
ISBN 0-8007-1201-3

TO husband, Bob,
and
son, David,
and
the kids at Covenant House,
New York City

Contents

Devil on the Deck

1

Death on the Footropes

The ship, a five-hundred ton East Indiaman, rode at anchor in the mouth of the Grand Canal, Venice. The water there was deep enough for any vessel. Just opposite was the church where Saint Mark lay buried for over seventeen centuries. Sails neatly snugged down, the *Dareway* lay folded in by fog and early morning mist. Johnny crouched low in the black gondola, smiling at the angry man who was sculling him out to the ship.

"You're no Peter Lodestone, you're not!" the man said hotly. "No doubt but you fly a different flag in every port! I mind me you were here two years ago, and then it was Maria Palozzi who cried her heart out. Then you were Charlie Breakwater! What's your *real* name?"

Johnny dropped his smile. "Drake, the pirate!" he snapped. "Keep your voice down, my good man. If you wake anyone, I'll pay my debts with the topsail and wish you a bad voyage back to your dirty canals!"

"My own cousin—our beautiful Floretta! You, with your

11

fair promises of marrying her and taking her back to England!
You, a low swab from a leaking merchant tub. A curse on all
seamen for your sake! A curse on your damp, mizzling, gouty
country! You will at least write to her?"

"Certainly—tomorrow." The boat glided up against the
ship's hull. "Do be still, you imbecile! Bear around to the port
side, now. Ah, there's the rope, and up top is my faithful
Steenie!"

A tarred rope snaked down, and Johnny twisted his left arm
in the loops and chinked money into the man's hand. "Good-
bye to sweet Maria!" he sang out softly.

"Floretta!" The gondolier shone the coins on his pants
then shook his fist at Johnny. "You've paid me in black dogs!
Counterfeit! Blast your eyes! Robber! Liar! Ho, captain!
Help—!"

His words were chopped off as Johnny's fist smacked his
teeth together, and the gondolier sprawled into the bottom of
his boat, his face one big, drooling puzzle.

"Be gone, you ugly water rat," Johnny said pleasantly.
Bracing his feet against the ship, he paced himself up the side,
hand over hand. A bushy gray head emerged at the top, a
square jaw clamped on a clay pipe, mild, brown reproachful
eyes. Faithful Steenie.

Steenie helped him climb over the bulwark. "Keep an eye
out for the watch. He's coming around now."

"Go below," Johnny muttered. "I've business to attend to."

Steenie vanished like steam from a teakettle. Johnny hauled
in the rope, draped it into a coil, and hid it in the tarp-covered
jolly boat. He watched the gondola until it was out of sight.
Groping his way across the wooden deck, his bare feet
knocked against the top of the ladder leading to the forecastle,
where the deckhands were quartered. He counted slowly up to
one hundred, then padded noiselessly down the steps. He
wanted to hear what they would say of him.

Steenie sat on the edge of his hammock, talking in a low
voice to the new hands, Ralph and Clarence, who had been

kidnapped, drugged, and carried on board two days ago. Old Burgoo, the cook, swung in his hammock, holding a burning candle.

"He's a con-ter-diction, Johnny is," said Steenie. "Marv'lous learning in his head, but two fists that work like hammer and anvil when he's in a temper, which is frequent. Aye, he has a dark fire locked in his breast, an evil secret. Says his ma died when he was seven, and him packed off to boarding school, a vicious place. Then he ran the streets with other young devils. He has his calms, and he has his storms, but blamed if I know the heart of the matter. Don't cross his trail if you can help it!"

The man called Ralph leaned forward to speak, and when Johnny heard his voice, he felt his pulses quit then race like a snared bird's heart.

"Is his surname *Newton?*" Ralph had to ask twice, and Johnny edged around a corner of the ladder until he could see Ralph's face. Blood! Curse the man! Was it possible?

"I know him," Ralph went on.

"Shipped together afore this?" Steenie asked.

"No, we—."

Clarence stood up in a hurry and stretched, his pale blond head bumping the beams.

"What's the ship carrying?"

Steenie eyed Ralph sharply, then turned to Clarence. "Salt, lace tablecloths, spices, gold, hides, perfume, vases, paintings, statues, glass. Seventy men on board."

"How's the pay?"

"Twenty-four shillings a month, and a little smuggling on the side, if you care to do it."

"How's she vittled?"

Steenie wiped his nose in a rag. "Oh, salt junk, cracker hash, dandy funk, slumgullion. The salt pork comes with long red wigglers in it, but just cast your eyes yonder when you eat, and you won't mind. Not much fresh water. You didn't bring knives or forks, I see, or extra clothing, so you had better buy some things from the slop chest."

"Without money?" Ralph protested.

Steenie went on, paying no notice to the interruption. "You'll need a donkey's breakfast—mattress stuffed with straw, you know—and some socks. You can pay in favors, same as us."

"Such as?"

"Such as taking an extra trick at the watch, staying here in *my* clothes if you ever get shore leave, and letting *me* go ashore in *your* clothes. Johnny'll set you a smart example there. Oh, there's ways. How'd you two get stranded in Venice, anyway?"

Ralph sighed. "A long story. . . ."

The candlelight fluttered over his flat, pock-marked face, and Johnny sucked in his breath and swore silently. The same! Yes, the very same! His old schoolmaster from West Essex Hall! Johnny felt his palms drip, his heart thud, and he was eight years old again, a terrified little boy standing before a most cruel teacher. The shock was like the old slaps across the face he remembered so well. Aye, he would always remember.

By thunder! He didn't have to fear him now! The villain! The weasel! Caught by a press gang, huh, and forced to sea? Served him right—a rare joke.

Johnny jumped down the last three steps, landing hard on both feet, jigged a few dance steps, whistled half a tune, and blew the candle out.

"Tuppence for the man who guesses who's come home to stay!" he cried.

Old Burgoo relit the candle with his flint. "You young cutthroat! I'll mince you up, I will! And where have you been off to these two days? Oh, you never *intend* to disgrace yourself; oh, no, not *you,* not your mother's son wot stands here afore me in the sinful flesh. Oh, no, I dare say you had not the *least thought* of disgracing yourself and the ship wot's home to you and your mates wot love you. Oh, *no!*"

Old Burgoo swung himself in the hammock with each word, until he was dizzy and panting. A wrinkled nightcap hid his bald head, and his little whiskered face perched atop a slightly humped body.

"Oh, no, my little sweetheart, you never *intend* to do wrong—oh, dear, not you! Oh, you'll grow up to be a credit to your country if you don't take care!"

Johnny ignored him and climbed into his own hammock. The fo'c'sle was a filthy hole down beneath the waterline of the ship, smelling of rancid butter and cheese, sour water, and chicken dung. Water sloshed underfoot even in fair weather. The men were never dry. Most of them lay asleep, a few yawning and writhing and grumbling to themselves.

Johnny looked at Ralph steadily, nonchalant. "Ever been on the briny before?"

The older man stared back at him somewhat fearfully. "Young John? So it *is* you. No, I imagine you know I've never been to sea. The press-gang—."

Johnny laughed scornfully. "They get every able man who isn't mighty quick on his feet. And our own judges upholding them and saying, 'Men of England, true blue, with hearts of oak, you ought to be glad to serve your country!' Where did they snatch you?"

"Right here in Venice. My brother and I were vacationing. Clarence is sickly. . . . I'm worried how he'll do. And you, Young John? It has been years—."

"Since I was eight years old? Aye, put another eight to it." Johnny shrugged and rolled over as if to sleep.

"Young John? You don't hold against me—anything?"

"Not I," Johnny lied promptly.

"And now you're before the mast, a regular seaman, adventuring, I suppose."

"Been seven voyages in the Mediterranean trade with my father, the commander," Johnny said airily. "He's retired, now, employed by Trinity House, surveying the tides. A good enough life for an old man."

Old Burgoo hopped out of the hammock and stuck the candle in Steenie's hand. "Oh, it ain't time for Old Burgoo yet. Oh, no, lads, we'll lay abed for the morning and have tea with the captain! Oh, we'll have a fine meal this love-a-ly morning, with hot cross buns and crumpets and a nice figgy-dowdy!"

The mention of fruit pudding made Johnny's stomach crawl. "Hurry along, you toad. And don't peach on me!"

"Give us a glim!" a man howled, and Steenie stood up and shone the light in his direction.

Old Burgoo disappeared into the galley, and in a short while Johnny smelled burned biscuit and oatmeal. He lined up with the men, and each one received two ladles full of watery oatmeal burgoo in his tin basin, two charred biscuits, and a mugful of water.

Johnny wolfed down his food. Out of the corner of his eye he watched the two brothers. His old schoolmaster ate the gruel like a spinster picking at her needlework. Clarence, thin as a matchstick, smelled the stuff, then gave it away to the nearest man. Johnny could have laughed until he cried. What an elegant pair! What a splendid voyage this would be!

The sun burst out of the sea like a proud lady, and the ship sprang into life. "All hands!" Captain Abell shouted, and the mates passed it on, and the bosun tweeted on his whistle. "All hands on deck! All hands!"

Ralph pressed against him as they climbed up the steps. "You really don't hold any hard feelings for those days that are past?" he asked anxiously. "There were so many hundreds of boys and so unruly, you know, that nothing but a strapping now and then would hold them."

"No hard feelings," Johnny said, looking him straight in the eyes, but his brain cried: *Wretch—brute—hypocrite!*

"A terrible life for Clarence," Ralph blurted as the men shoved and lined up on deck. He stuck close to Johnny. "He's not at all well. He might not survive this."

"All hands!" Captain Abell, in smart blue uniform and cocked hat, glared directly at them, then snapped open his little black book and read prayers. This done, the men scattered for work. The tide was turning, and the men at the capstan strained against the spokes, ready to turn the wheel and weigh the anchor.

"Riggers aloft!" bellowed the captain, and the order was echoed by the officers. Johnny leaped into the rigging and went up like a monkey. He was proud to be in charge of the topgallant sail of the foremast, the highest sail except one.

"Yardsmen lay aloft and loose the fore t'ga'nt sail," the officer below yammered in a monotone as though he were reciting the alphabet. "Man the fore t'ga'nt sail sheets and halyard. Tend the lee brace, let fall, lay in and overhaul gear, throw off the buntlines. . . ."

Johnny worked with five other men, bare toes gripping the tarry ratlines underfoot, then swaying on a single rope, almost fifteen stories' height above the deck. All the spars were thick with men, like roosting fowl.

". . . Ease the clew lines, throw off the royal sheets, sheet home, and belay!"

The canvas dropped in loose folds and bellied out, full breasted. The capstan hands chanted as they hauled up the anchor, and the fiddler, squatting on the capstan in the center, plied his bow most violently. Up came the five-ton anchor, a dead weight dangling on thick rope cables.

Johnny stopped to draw breath and ease the ache in his side and wipe his blistered hands on his cotton pants. He looked down. The *Dareway* was as beautiful, he thought, as perfect and unwrinkled as a painting on silk. She was a white gull mounted on a polished sapphire. He was master now, master of the mast, of the ship, the sea, the world, on this bouncing blue day.

A spook-thin breeze teased the topsail and whispered down the mast. The sails angled around, and she was moving. Stronger wind in the powerful sails moulded them like iron. Johnny tasted the same rise of excitement every time he smelled salty sea and felt the ship rise and fall and knew each day would be full of emergencies, each port full of girls, hours snatched in the afternoon for reading books.

"September, seventeen forty-three," he said. "We are going home!" Home meant England, and he had almost forgotten he had no other home except a ship.

Four days outward bound and they ran into a storm. In late afternoon Johnny was lounging amidship with Steenie, sipping his grog ration and complaining. "What watery slop. Will we get limes tomorrow, Burgoo? I'll squeeze mine in the grog and make a little flavor."

Old Burgoo leaned over the rail, staring ahead. "Storm," he grunted. "I can smell it. See the water change color? This one'll be a *bad* one!"

Ralph and Clarence, on their free time, looked to Steenie for a comment. "You don't see bad weather, do you?"

Steenie removed his pipe from his dog-shaped jaws, patted his curly gray head, and looked thoughtful. Finally he said, "There's a squall ahead, or my name ain't Austin Handwick. Burgoo is right. I can *smell* it!"

Clarence shuffled his feet nervously. "Can we go below? I wouldn't know what to do. I wouldn't be any help in a storm."

"That's when a man learns," Johnny said quickly. "You stick close to me, Ralph's Brother, and I'll teach you some ropes. Only three hundred to learn. You'll make a jolly good rigger, trust me."

"In the rigging in a storm?" Ralph said angrily. "And him only four days at sea?"

"A storm at sea, a storm for tea," Old Burgoo croaked. "Oh, my poor little ones, what a pity. Old Burgoo was fixing such a love-a-ly supper for ye, trussed up piglet, apples and suet pudding, sweet yams and date cakes." He danced in a tight circle, sawing on an imaginary fiddle. "Fiddle-de-dee and hey nonnie-no, dance for your supper, children, dance in the rigging, for that's all ye'll get tonight!"

"The sky is bright blue," Johnny protested, "and your head ain't worth a secondhand sieve. I say you're wrong. I ought to know weather. I say the queen's great-aunt Tillie could sail this washtub!"

The mate strolled over, calling to them, "Barometer's falling, lads, be prepared."

Johnny shut his mouth in surprise. Ralph said, "We're green sticks, Young John, but we'll do our duty."

"Come aloft with me, Ralph's Brother."

"I'll do my share," Clarence offered slowly.

A single rain cloud came over the horizon; then within five minutes rain clouds, purple, ugly, leering, piled up like castle walls, tumbling down again. The waves threw up white tips, and the sudden storm breeze was like a long drink of cold water.

"All hands!" The rigging sang in the whining wind. The men, roused out of naps and card games, swarmed over the deck to their positions.

"Dirty weather, this!" Steenie shouted in Johnny's ear. "Watch out for the two lubbers!"

Johnny braced his feet to roll with the ship and grinned. He'd been in worse storms. About time the schoolmaster and his pukey brother got their sea legs! Yes, indeed. He would see to it.

"Reef sails! Look sharp!" the mate screamed. "Riggers aloft! Move, you blasted pirates!"

Slanting sheets of rain hit them. The mainmast began to trace circles against the black clouds. The clouds butted the ship from all sides. Lightning sizzled down the mizzenmast; the royal sail took fire and burned out.

"Follow me!" Johnny put his mouth to Clarence's ear. He forced the man ahead of him as he climbed up on the ratlines. Boiling black clouds draped around them, and Johnny shoved Clarence higher. Together they reached the mainsail, passed it, higher to the lower topsail, up to the upper topsail, to the topgallant. There was a lull in the storm, and Clarence cried, "I can't walk the footrope, never did before!"

Johnny smiled widely through his beard. He could see Ralph below, coming after them, the mate shaking his fist, Old Burgoo flying headfirst down the stairway, Steenie directly

across on the mizzenmast, flat on his belly on the yard to hold
the sail down.

"Belay!" roared the mate through a speaking trumpet, but
the wind caught the word away as soon as he spoke it.

Johnny stepped out on the footrope slung beneath the yardarm and motioned Clarence to follow him. Clarence's face was
white as flour, and he swayed dangerously and walked sideways on the rope like a crab.

The ship began to pitch in the driving sea. Clarence leaned
across the yardarm and vomited. The ship reared like a bang-
tailed horse, and Johnny calmly rocked with it, holding to the
spar with one hand. One man on the upper topsail accidentally
wound his shirttail up in the sails and hung there, kicking, in
the driving rain.

Steenie was in trouble, Johnny saw. The sail bucked out of
his hands, snapped to the left, and with a screaming rip blew
clean away.

The ship fought hard for her life; the rigging creaked and
groaned; the wind hammered Johnny's head like the endless
roll of a drumbeat, but he loved it all. His sail properly furled,
he was ready to climb down. Clarence was still belly down on
the yard, and Johnny shook his arm. "Come along, Ralph's
Brother! She's all right now! Fine job!"

Clarence didn't move, and Johnny pounded on his back.
"Go down backwards, same as you got up! Go along, now! I'll
make an able seaman out of you yet!"

Clarence forced himself up straight, but his eyes were closed
and his hands soldered fast on the yard.

Johnny was a little alarmed. Why, the silly fellow meant to
take up housekeeping here, married to the mast and to bed in
the crow's nest. "Go down, you fool!" he yelled. "Down!
Clarence! Wake up!"

Clarence rolled his eyes up in his head, loosened his death
grip, and fell headfirst down to the deck. Johnny saw the red
strawberry spot far below before a wave washed the deck
clean. He was shaky, then sourly sick, but wiped his mouth and

scrambled down the ratlines. The storm had passed over, and he dropped to the deck, landing in knee-high black water and wreckage of barrels. The dead man had been carried below, but Steenie and Ralph waited for him.

"Broke all his bones," said Steenie quietly.

Johnny didn't answer. His lips were suddenly too loose, unable to form words, and his innards all awash. The first mate half slid, half swam through the water, and his huge fist, the size of a ham, cracked Johnny's ear. "Get aloft to the topmast crosstrees!" he shrilled. "Get aloft and stay there until I call for you, you young devil! You pup! After that, the captain will see you flogged!"

The ship still pitched and tossed, and the sky remained dark. *That storm may yet come back* was Johnny's only thought as he pulled his aching body up the shroud ropes.

Ralph attacked him, clean out of his head, blind with rage cursing and raving, tears filling all the little holes in his face.

Johnny heard only his final words before Steenie dragged him away: "A man can't drown who's born to be hung!"

2

The Mysterious Ring

The dream was so strange that Johnny wrote it all down when he awoke, so he would always remember it.

A week after Clarence's death he dreamed the ship was still anchored in the Grand Canal at Venice, sails clewed up for the night.

In the fourth watch of the night, he paced the deck alone, grateful for the cool air that soothed his sore back. He was lucky to get off with twenty lashes. Steenie had lied and said Clarence was determined to go aloft to prove his mettle.

The flood of moonlight through the rigging cast a magic of shadows on the deck. Midnight, and the mate from the quarterdeck sang out, "Eight bells!"

Johnny all of a sudden sensed he was being observed. Circling around smartly, he looked into the dark corners of the deck—behind the hatches, along the raised poop deck, under the bulwark railing.

"Aha! I have you!" Nothing but a rat from the watery hold of the ship. The ship, like a giant bucket of lard, wallowed lazily. The bow rose and fell gently with the mild push of water.

All at once a ball of fire bounded along the horizon, then leaped lightly to the foremast, the mainmast, the mizzenmast. Johnny opened his mouth to cry, "Fire!" then remembered. Ball lightning! This was only the second time in his life he had seen it. Ball lightning was scary but harmless.

Now he heard nothing but the soft cat tread of his feet. He saw the North Star and the other stars like millions of fiery specks. A half-dozen men lay curled up in the giant coils of rope in the stern of the ship, sound asleep.

"Good evening!"

Johnny spun around on one bare foot. His hand flew to the knife in his belt. But he felt no fear, instead a gradual peace filled his heart. He didn't pull the knife.

A Person stood by him on the deck, just a glowing outline of a figure. Johnny could not see a face, and he dared not ask for a name.

"I have something for you, Johnny, if you'll accept it."

Johnny bent over the outstretched hand and saw a heavy, gold, man's ring with a design on it, the kind of ring rulers and kings used to seal their letters. Johnny had read about the practice of folding a letter, dripping a bit of hot wax on the fold, then pressing the design of the ring into the wax. This was the way rich men signed letters.

"Aye, I'd like to have it," Johnny said boldly. "A stolen ring, no doubt."

He felt, rather than saw, his new Friend smile.

"No, Johnny. While you wear this ring, you will be happy and have much success. If you lose it or part with it, you will have trouble and unhappiness."

Johnny slipped the ring on his middle finger and wondered that it fit snugly. "My thanks," he said. "I like this, I do. I'm the master of my own happiness and comfort. Wouldn't I be a fool to part with the ring? It shall never come off my finger; I can promise you that."

He felt, rather than saw, the sadness of the Person. When he looked up he saw only the bone white moon. *Weird as a fetch-*

light that witches carry, he thought. But the ring was still there on his finger, solid gold, with its curious design.

He took a few turns about the deck, congratulating himself on his good luck and the idea that he was now ruler of his life. Opposite the mizzenmast he heard a movement. His heart skipped beats. Someone was there. That Person again?

No. Into the moonlight strolled a tall, handsome fellow in evening dress, hat, and walking cane. A handsome devil, that. Maybe a gentleman from ashore. Strange, he didn't know the ship carried passengers.

"Good evening."

"Evening," Johnny responded. There was something he didn't quite like about the man. A handsome devil, though, not much older than himself.

"I couldn't help taking note of your ring," said the man. Johnny tried to see his face, but it was in the shadow. "A beautiful ring, if I may be so bold. I could see it gleaming in the moonlight. A gentleman's ring. A wealthy man's ring. You are the captain's son?"

"N-no," said Johnny, though the idea occurred to him that with the ring he could probably be the captain if he chose.

"A young merchant, then," said the man in black. "Ah, yes, that's it. And I see you are also educated and clever."

Confound the man, but he was deep! Johnny rather liked him now. He laid his bare arm along the bulwark railing and admired the ring. Four letters were carved on top, but he couldn't quite make out the word.

"As long as I wear the ring I shall be happy and prosperous," he said proudly. "This ring makes me master over my life and my fortune. I can be anything now. A very wonderful Person gave me the ring."

"Did he really?" The man's voice grew cold. "A sort of mysterious figure, was he, gliding around and in disguise? Halting in the shadows and not saying overly much? Ah, yes, I know him."

Johnny shifted his arm, a little uncomfortable. "You mean the ring isn't—?"

"Oh, dear, yes, it is gold, beyond the shadow of a doubt. Priceless! But don't you see what that rascal has done to you?"

Johnny gazed at him earnestly. A handsome devil, he was, a real man of the world. He seemed to understand Johnny and know what was best for him.

"I don't know what you mean," he said finally. "Will the ring cause me harm?"

The stranger didn't answer directly. "Don't you see that you are not master of yourself at all? You are trusting a silly bit of jewelry, a ring on your finger. Oh, it's not fake, he's too clever for that. But to trust in a magic ring—oh, it's just too foolish, like the boy in the fairy tale!" The fellow fell to laughing and nearly split the buttons from his vest.

"But he said—"

"Did he really? What exactly did he say?"

"While I wear the ring I will be happy and—and—," Johnny found it difficult to remember. He had felt so comfortable in His presence.

". . . and find pots of gold at the rainbow and be captain of a great ship and own a palace with servants and marry the princess? Oh, it's such a marvelous joke!" The handsome devil chuckled so, Johnny wondered the whole crew didn't hear and come running.

"You just want my ring," he said angrily. "You expect to buy my gold ring for about half what it's worth! Do you think I haven't sailed the seas and haven't met thieves and cheats before this?"

"My dear boy, consider what you are saying!" The dark stranger turned angry. "I can tell you I have thousands—no, millions—of rings like that! Yes, I own them, they are mine! To think that you are afraid to face life without a bit of jewelry, like a silly, weak girl! Afraid to stand on your own two feet!"

Johnny swung at him with his fist, but his fist seemed to pass through air. At the same time he shouted: "Afraid, am I? I'm not afraid of anything! I'll show you I don't need a ring! But *you* won't have the ring—oh, no!"

Johnny forced the ring from his finger, shot back his right arm, then threw with all his strength. The ring spun up in a high arch, sparkling in the moonlight, then fell swiftly, terribly, into the endless deeps of the sea.

The figure beside him broke into wild laughter, crying, "Thank you! Thank you!" and at the same time Johnny whirled around to stare in horror at the shoreline of the city of Venice and the Alps mountains behind it, which were aflame with fire. He heard the helpless crackle and crack of the trees and smelled the charred smoke. A wall of fire ate up the helpless city, then flowed out over the harbor, raging out of control, closer, closer, until he felt lapped around by the intense heat. Now his hair, his shirt, his pants were on fire. He was breathing fire! He tried to scream, but his mouth stuck shut.

The creature in black hugged himself with delight as he danced about on the deck. "Ha, ha, ha, ha! Don't you understand now? The fire hisses and burns just for you! You are mine and must go with me to the mountains of fire! Come along!"

"The ring!" Johnny wrung his hands together in despair. Oh, if only he had the ring!

"It's too late! Didn't you see the word graven on the ring? S-o-u-l, *soul!* You have thrown away your soul! Come along! Come along!"

"No—no—oh, God! God, help me!"

A wall of gobbling flame rolled toward him, crimson red, evil blue, yellow sparks, cinders and ashes flying in his eyes.

"God!"

Then, a miracle. The first Person he had met stood by him, and Johnny felt a moment of coolness and relief. "Johnny, what has happened?"

"Oh, what a fool I have been. Oh, curse me for a fool! I threw away the ring, the ring that might have saved me. Gone

forever! Don't even pity me or come near me! I've ruined myself! There's no hope for me! Oh, God!"

The Person touched his arm. "You are right. You do not deserve any pity, for you threw away the ring of your own free
will. Johnny, if you had the ring back, would you be any wiser
this time?"

Johnny couldn't reply, for he could not tear his gaze away
from the awful scene of heat and torment. He couldn't shake
off the knowledge that he belonged to the wicked man in black,
who held him in his arms and began to pull him toward the
mountains.

When he was finally able to turn his head about to the
ocean, he saw his Friend dive under the water at the very spot
where the ring had fallen. Drowned! No, in another second the
Person stood behind him, the ring shining on his outstretched
hand. That moment the man in black vanished, the fires were
doused, and Johnny reached for the ring.

"No." The Person gently closed his own hand on the ring,
hiding it from view. "No, Johnny, the ring is safe. But if I give
it to you, the same thing might happen again. I will keep the
ring safe for you. Should you ever need help, call me, for I will
surely answer."

He disappeared, and Johnny woke up. He was crouched on
his hands and knees in his hammock, his face buried in the
hemp. His joints were stiff with fear and his head dizzy. He
couldn't move until Steenie, below, rocked the hammock and
coaxed him out. Old Burgoo dashed some water in his face,
and the men crowded around.

"He's had a scare, he has," said Steenie. "Been dreaming.
Come, Johnny, look alive, we're here and it's all right. Come,
now, lad, have some vittles and drink."

"Oh, he's had a warnin' from above, has our Johnny, I sees it
written all over his face!" Old Burgoo singsonged, hanging
over him and fanning his face with somebody's broken shoe.

"Our Johnny sometimes ain't all a young'un should be, but

he's got marv'lous learnin' in his head, and when he sneaks ashore, he does bring us back treats, a nice round of cheese oncet, and—"

"Stop your nonsense!" Steenie commanded, punching the cook in the chest.

"It would be fitting if the evil one carried him off," Ralph said bitterly, rolling around in his bunk, searching for a scarf to tie on his head.

Johnny sat up awkwardly, dazed and still very much afraid. He desperately wished to go on deck and look toward Venice and see if the fire was really doused. Then it came back to him. They were well on their way to England in the middle of the Mediterranean Sea. It was only a dream.

The dream didn't wear off as other dreams do. Johnny found himself clenching and unclenching his left hand where the ring had been—where he thought—dreamed—the ring had been. He kept glancing down at his left hand. He couldn't eat and took only watery grog when Steenie offered it. For three days the captain excused him from work and sent him below. He overheard Steenie talking to Captain Abell.

"Captain, sir, you mind how Johnny seems absent from us, sir. I'm wondering if Mister Bones—I mean the ship's doctor, and begging pardon, sir—I'm wondering if he mightn't know of some remedy for Johnny's state of mind, sir. Clarence's death was a shock, sir, and that I do believe has worked upon his mind so that it keeps coming back."

"Rightly so, Handwick, wouldn't you say?" the captain replied shrewdly. "That lad puts a curse on a ship. I won't have him again. I'd sooner go aloft myself than have that bad one on my ship." The captain patted his velvet coat lapels for emphasis and fussed with the gold buttons. "Yes, Handwick, I do believe I'd go aloft before I'd see my ship jinxed again." He lifted his telescope and peered out to leeward. "Mighty nice weather, this."

"Captain, sir, I do believe his mind might not come back unless he's seen to, sir," Steenie persisted.

"Indeed, Handwick, you take too much upon yourself. Are you his father? I know his father. An upright and God-fearing man, though some call him cold and stern. Educated in Spain, he was. Commander Newton has my respect. He did nothing to deserve such a son, an ungrateful, lazy, mischief-maker, a ne'er-do-well. . . ." The captain ran out of words and took up his sextant to "shoot the sun," first spitting over the side for good luck.

"Mr. Cleaver, write down our position." The quartermaster obeyed, and the captain turned to go below. "I shall write an account of this voyage to his father. My conscience would niggle at me if I didn't tell of the—accident. Take advice from your captain, Austin Handwick. That boy has no conscience, and I'd be pleased to see you put your spare time to better use."

Johnny ducked behind the mast. The mention of his father was like a blow in the face. Yes, soon he would have to face him. Johnny began to think of what excuses he could give for not wanting to return to sea. The bad dream faded away. More practical things demanded attention. Like how to find a soft job where he could read all day long, work sums, which delighted his mind, or just sit and daydream life away.

He joined a couple of hands sunning themselves and yarning on the starboard side. A fellow named Ned was talking. "War with France, soon, I can feel it in my bones."

"War over what quarrel?" Johnny asked quickly.

"West Indies—or Canada—or both."

Limpy knocked his pipe against the bulwark. "Seen a man cut through the middle and roasted alive with chain shot. That's yer French—heat their loads red-hot, you know. They're not just cannonballs, neither, oh, no! They're sharp iron, all nasty points and swinging hooks. Just one chain shot can snag a topsail and rip 'er down!"

Johnny shivered. He'd always had the fear of the press-gang getting him on board a man-of-war. Even small boys were used as powder monkeys to deliver the highly explosive shells from one deck to another. A slip, a fall, and the boy would be blown into pieces.

Oh, the man-of-war was a h— ship all right. Of course a merchant ship was armed with cannon, also, to protect the ship against pirates, but in the Mediterranean it was rarely necessary to defend the ship.

A real man-of-war carried forty-eight big guns and six cannon and could make eleven knots in the wind. The discipline was brutal. The risk of being mutilated always frightened Johnny. He knew a ship's surgeon was quick to amputate. When at sea with his father, he had seen a screaming man held down on the midshipmen's dining table while the chaplain poured liquor down his throat to dull the pain and the surgeon sawed his leg off with a dull blade.

Ned almost read his thoughts. "Aye, a h— ship. I saw a man-o'-war blow up. First we heard a hissing, then came the explosion. the ship jerked herself up from the water, the masts blew sky high, and she sank in two minutes. Two minutes," he repeated solemnly. "Her powder magazine exploded. Sky red for nigh an hour."

Chips, the carpenter, said, "Not many things worse, to my mind, than a three-ton gun breaking loose and having the run of the deck. I saw a loose cannon roll over three men, break their legs, then smash right through the bulwark and down into the briny."

Ned had sandy hair, hollows under his eyes, and a peg for a nose, but he was intelligent, Johnny decided. "Shipped around the Horn," he was saying, "and up the Spanish Main. Caught in a hurricane, and she made water so fast we lived like dead men, stuck tight to our posts, never eating, never a drop of water, just our arms churning and our chests near bursting and the deck rolling—rolling—and we never saw daylight or got dry for almost twenty-two days. Men dropped dead at the pumps. She was naught but a wreck when we spied the coast of Chile, with twenty-four men dead. Rats sold at four shillings apiece; we were that hungry."

Johnny regarded him with wonder. "How long have you been at sea?"

"Five years. Before that I was a master at school, like Ralph here. I like life at sea, though, and I like to read. I couldn't abide school life. I'm not a cruel man, but I was forced to be cruel to keep order. Do you believe, I'd rather work four hours on and four off, as we do here, than be a schoolmaster?"

Johnny looked at him with new respect. "I think I have seen you reading up in the crow's nest."

Ned grinned widely. "Nay, lad, don't pass the word around. Captain Abell has good ears."

"Oh, I wouldn't peach. What do you read?"

The other men wedged them out of their little circle, but Johnny didn't care. He wanted to talk to Ned. "I have been reading since I was three years old," he said, boasting. "At four, I read great books."

"What books?"

Johnny's tongue stumbled over the words, and he was ashamed. "I—I read from the Bible, from hymnbooks and poems," he said, face flushing. "Oh, it didn't mean anything to me. I don't believe such stuff."

Ned surprised him. "Why, I think that was fine, Johnny. I think that was a fine beginning."

"Do you, now? I remember I could repeat whole chapters from that—that Book. Of course it was dreadfully old-fashioned, you know. I much prefer adventures."

Ned had a hearty laugh. "Only natural to like adventure stories. What else?"

"When I was six I read Latin."

Ned beamed, and Johnny thought him the most delightful fellow he ever met and wondered why he had not met him sooner. "You surely did not learn all that in a school, now?"

"No, my—my mother taught me at home. She—died—when I was seven."

"Awfully hard on you," Ned said gently.

Johnny turned his head away and was silent for a few minutes. Finally he said, "Aye."

"Then I suppose you were sent to boarding school and forgot all you learned."

"How did you know?" Johnny gaped at him.

"I told you, I was a master and know those schools. Horrid places."

"My father married again, and I had a stepmother. Not that she was mean to me, just that—well, she soon had her own baby and sent me off to school. The master was rotten—I hated him—we all did. And I wanted so much to study, but I wasn't happy."

Ned stretched out his stubby legs and ironed his pants with his hands. "Of course not. How could you be happy there?"

"I was reading Tully and Vergil when I was nine years old," Johnny said eagerly. "I loved it so much. Then when I turned eleven my father thought his money was wasted at that school and took me to sea."

"What's he like, your father?"

Johnny fell silent. His father. How could he describe him, or even talk about him? He couldn't. Ned didn't force him. They just sat and enjoyed the silence and the slight rocking of the ship and the sunshine.

Ned spoke first. "I'm reading a smallish, thin book with the odd title of *Rhapsody*."

Johnny's face lit up. "I read that long ago. Picked it up in Holland one year. We must discuss it sometime."

The watch changed, and the men scrambled to their feet and went to work, some mending sails, some splicing ropes, others scraping and painting the ship.

Johnny worked as hard as any. He didn't want to think anymore about the silly dream—or meeting his father.

3

The Girl From Maidstone

Johnny arrived back in England the first week in December, and his father met him in Liverpool. They took a carriage to the Lion's Head Inn, where Johnny stuffed himself with roast beef, sausages, boiled potatoes, a meat pie, pudding, and two glasses of wine.

He was feeling warm and sleepy and perfectly content to do and be nothing, when his father began to talk.

Mr. Newton was tall and bulky, but neatly dressed in gray knee breeches, a black coat with gray muffler, and leather boots. Johnny glanced into the glittering mirrors opposite and compared the two images. He looked the part of the poor sailor boy just home, with his patched cotton shirt and pants, his greatcoat too short in the sleeves, and his untrimmed brown hair and beard.

His father also studied the two images, then said, "Now, sir, we will purchase a proper suit and boots for you, before any of my friends think I'm befriending a pirate."

Johnny didn't laugh, because his father's remarks were meant to hurt.

"You will also visit the barber," Mr. Newton continued. "By the by, I have Captain Abell's letter in hand. And to say I am displeased would not register with you, no doubt, but I am at a loss what to do with you, sir."

Johnny mumbled something about "that green stick *would* go aloft, no matter how I tried to stop him," but his father's cold eyes bored through him, and he gave up.

"Since you are determined never to try and raise your position on ship," his father said wearily, "I asked my good friend, Mr. Joseph Manesty, a merchant, to take you to Jamaica with him for five years and teach you his business. Perhaps he can do what I seem to have failed to do." Mr. Newton allowed himself a slight sigh and looked down at his plate.

"Yes, sir," Johnny replied from force of habit. Jamaica? Yes, an island in the West Indies. The weather was always warm there. Jamaica wouldn't be so bad—prime swimming, fishing, idleness. And time to read! "Yes, sir, I'd like Jamaica!"

His father frowned and pierced him through with his steely eyes. "Would you now?" he sneered. "I can read your mind, sir, and I know what you are thinking. Mr. Manesty, you know, is very strict with his people. You'll have no idle life, sunning on the beaches and reading storybooks. You are going to learn the merchant business!"

"Yes, sir." Johnny tried to speak humbly. Drat the man, he was deep, he was. "This time I'll try hard. Just don't put me back on a ship for good."

"Mr. Manesty is doing me a grand favor. His ship sails three days from today. Now that I reflect, you won't need new clothes. Come back to my lodging with me and you'll find last year's suit and greatcoat. The boots may be tight, but in three days you'll be on board ship, and I'll have saved money. Do go to the barber, though; I can't abide ragged hair."

Just like you, Johnny thought bitterly. *Oh, I'll go to Jamaica all right, and I'll have myself a fine time, too, once I'm out of sight.*

"I still remember when you were but fifteen," his father

continued. "You had a fine chance to better yourself in Alicant, Spain, but you wasted your time and took up with the wrong sort of friends." He gazed over Johnny's head, coldly. "This is your last and final chance to make something of your life. Mr. Manesty has offered to be a father to you."

Johnny resolved to hate Mr. Manesty. "Yes, sir," he mouthed.

"Now, sir," his father said, rising from the table, "I have an errand for you after you change clothes. Take this letter to Mr. Alfred Beekman, a white house on Clove Road, two miles beyond Maidstone in Kent. Very easy to find, if you keep on the old post road. I'll expect you back Thursday morning, for the ship sails early with the tide." He paid the gloomy waiter, who stood licking his fingers, then handed Johnny a key and a card. "Here is my lodging, and here is the key. Change into winter clothing and leave the key with Mrs. Kettering, next door. Mind you lock the door behind you. I'm off to an appointment now."

And a rousing good homecoming this is, thought Johnny bitterly. Aloud he said, "A fine meal, and I thank you, sir. I will be back on time."

"Remember that Mr. Beekman lives two miles beyond Maidstone, where the Catletts live."

Catletts! Mrs. Catlett took care of his mother when she lay dying. Johnny felt a sort of pain in his heart and a desire to see the old home again. "May I stop and bid farewell to Mrs. Catlett, sir?"

His father put all the tips of his fingers together to form a church steeple and didn't answer at once. "Yes, why not spend a few moments with Mrs. Catlett? Just don't waste any time."

"Thank you, sir." Johnny disposed of his father with a shrug, went out into the snowy streets, found the lodging, and struggled into his old winter clothes. "Not even in style," he muttered, peering into the mirror.

Locking the door behind him, he dropped off the key to Mrs. Kettering and hailed the mail coach for Kent. He slept all the way, until the driver bawled out, "Maidstone! Crossroads! All passengers out!"

Johnny found himself on a dirt road, with the wind pitchforking snow into drifts. Already his face and fingertips were stiff with the cold. He'd never be able to walk two miles before nightfall. Why not stay at Catletts' overnight and deliver the letter tomorrow?

He found the house, timidly knocked, and the huge door was swung open by a plump, motherly woman who first stared, then cried, "Johnny! Why, it's Johnny Newton, back from sea!" She hugged him over and over, took his hat and coat, and fussed over him, pulling him close to the big fireplace and its warmth.

Johnny rubbed his chapped hands together and grew cheerful. Aye, now he'd brag up his life at sea and give these country people something to wonder at. Aye, now *this* was a proper welcome!

All the gears in his head ground to a halt—stunned. A girl had stepped wonderingly into the room and gazed at him with a little fear in her eyes. A girl with a waterfall of honey-colored hair falling below her waist, a girl who didn't even reach his shoulder—why she wasn't more than thirteen or fourteen years old—a girl with eyes like the sea and dark brown eyelashes so thick they appeared tangled. A muffin-small nose, a stubborn little mouth, a pink frock with foolish daisies on it. . . . But her eyes! Johnny couldn't turn away. He was powerless. A line from an old book floated through his head. ". . . their souls were knit. . . ."

"Gracious me, come away from the fire. You're turning red as a lobster!" Mrs. Catlett laughingly steered him to the table. "Don't you remember Mary? Our Polly, we call her. No, you wouldn't. She was four and you were seven when she went off to school. And Catherine, here, was not even thought of!"

Johnny stared stupidly at the little girl in pale green. "Catherine?"

"My sister," said Polly softly. Her voice was scarcely more than a sweet whisper.

Johnny clumsily ate mince pie and cursed himself for a fool. Why couldn't he have bought new clothes? Why didn't he stop at the barber as he was told? Why hadn't he shaved off the sideburns? Enough to frighten country folk. Why were his hands so big and ugly, and why did he feel so stupid, and why couldn't he look up at those eyes again?

"More milk," said Mrs. Catlett, pouring another mugful. "More pie, too. I fancy you're starved after ship life. You'll stay a while, Johnny, a week or so, won't you?"

Yes, Johnny thought nervously, mashing up the pie with his fork, *I'll stay here a while, yes, indeed, I'll stay.*

"Mr. Catlett has taken to his bed with the gout," Mrs. Catlett said. "You can meet him in the morning. Grandpa still lives with us. Old as the sea he is, but still active. How is your father, Johnny?"

"He's well." Johnny could hardly swallow the pie crust, his mouth was that dry.

"And—and your stepmother?"

"I don't know. I didn't see her."

Silence fell until Polly broke it. "Have you come from the Indies?"

Johnny forced himself to look at her. "No, this time it was Venice." Gad! She was the most beautiful girl he had ever seen, a little woman already, homespun, but shy and cautious. Something in her eyes held him steady. They gazed at each other, and for a moment there was an understanding between them; then it was broken as little Catherine climbed into his lap, begging, "Tell us an adventure, Johnny."

"Tomorrow," Mrs. Catlett said, clearing the table. "Polly, love, put fresh candles upstairs. Catherine, take yourself off to sleep. Johnny needs a good night's rest in a feather bed before he can talk."

Johnny slept like a dead man, and it was almost noon when he woke. He donned the warm sweater Mrs. Catlett had kindly left on a chair and pulled on his trousers and socks. His sailor feet ached in the stiff leather boots when he walked downstairs.

Catherine skipped up to him. "You walk funny, from side to side."

"I've had to straddle a rolling deck," he replied and looked around for Polly.

She was laying the table for dinner, and today-she wore pale blue with a little white apron. Blue made her eyes look deep green, Johnny decided. Her thick, gold curls were pulled behind her ears and tied with a ribbon.

"M-morning, Mrs. Catlett and Polly," he stammered. Curse it, why couldn't he act natural? He felt like an overgrown cow. Polly poured from a monstrous china teapot, and Johnny held the tiny teacup in his big, callused hand and hated himself. He knew he was suntanned as an Indian, while she was all pink and creamy. His arms were thick and knotted with muscle, while she was tiny and perfect and smelled sweeter than vanilla.

Think of her as a sister, he warned himself. *Be careful.*

After dinner they sat around the fireplace, and Mr. Catlett fired questions at him. The name of the ship, the tonnage, her master, the cargo, the ports of call, until Johnny grew weary and began to yawn.

"Maybe I need a breath of air," he apologized. "Not used to indoor life, you know." It occurred to him that he and Polly might walk in the snow.

"Polly, show Johnny the barn and the new lambs," Mrs. Catlett came to the rescue. "Catherine, you may go with them."

Johnny silently groaned his disappointment.

"Bundle up, dears." Mrs. Catlett wound Mr. Catlett's muffler around Johnny's neck.

Polly looked adorable in a red wool bonnet edged in fur, long red cloak, and a fur muff for her hands. A regular sweetheart. Maybe he could help her through the snow and take her hand.

The sun shone after the snowstorm, the world sparkled; the path to the barn was short and the lambs sweet and appealing.

Johnny saw only Polly. *I must* get a promise from her, he thought. *Something to give me hope until—*

"May I write to you?" The hay around them in the barn smelled like summer, and the two cows rustled in their stalls.

"Y-yes." She wasn't exactly encouraging.

"And will you read my letters?"

She looked up at him, surprised. "Of course. We will all read your letters."

"I mean—will you answer my letters?"

Polly turned to walk back to the house. Such a short walk. Such a few minutes he'd had with her. "I don't know," she whispered.

Curse himself for a fool! He'd frightened her. She wasn't yet fourteen. "I've had some marvelous adventures," he said boldly. "Almost all over the world, taken by pirates, found treasure, watched glassblowing in Venice, seen all the jewelry fine ladies wear. Oh, you can't imagine, Polly, the stories I can tell—of—of Spanish castles, and islands, and shipwrecks." He was lying now, but she was listening. "I don't have time now to tell it, but I could write about it."

She looked at him gravely. "Do you like to write? And read?"

"Oh, surely. I read all the time on board ship." They reached the back porch, and the steps were slippery, so it was only natural for her to take his arm. He was careful to ignore it. "I'll write all about a sailor's life at sea, Polly. The terrible things that happen, the suffering; you can't imagine!"

She was wide-eyed now, and he couldn't stop. "I've fallen overboard, been beaten, worked until I fell down unconscious, starved!"

Inside, by the stone fireplace again, he saw pity in her face, and her lips parted as she leaned forward to listen to his story. The fire burned her cheeks rosy, but she seemed not to notice.

The next day Mrs. Catlett's sister, Mrs. Little, came to visit, and Johnny couldn't help hearing some of the conversation.

"As handsome as any," Mrs. Catlett said proudly. "They're

young, but he has ambition, and he'll captain a ship some day, mark my words."

"A captain of an East Indiaman makes ten thousand pounds a year," said Mrs. Little in admiring tones. "There's plenty of time yet. They're young. You are certain of his feeling for the girl?"

Mrs. Catlett bent over her sewing. "Oh, my, yes. Very evident. You know, his dear mother and I discussed this when they were mere infants. She was anxious to see his future settled with a nice girl from a churchgoing family. And no man could find a better girl than our Polly."

"Lovely—," agreed Mrs. Little, and he heard no more as the doors to the sitting room caught a draft and blew shut.

Days passed quickly, and after a week Mrs. Catlett said, "You needn't be in a hurry, Johnny. When are you due back to your ship?"

"Not for a week," he lied. And when she asked him the same question a week later, he gave the same answer. Altogether, three weeks passed, and he feared greatly when he thought of his father and the ship that sailed to Jamaica without him.

Gone were his boyish dreams of basking in the sun and living an idle life. Now he must find work so he would have something to offer Polly when he asked for her hand in marriage. He'd hurry back to his father, beg his forgiveness, plead for another chance to go into business. But take a five-year voyage? Never! Never!

The day he said good-bye to Polly was the most miserable day of his life. If Polly loved him, she gave no hint of it, but she was very quiet. Twice she had refused to attend a party at the home of friends. She listened, instead, to more of his sea tales around the fire.

On the last day he saw her alone for a few minutes while she was in the kitchen, baking cookies. Catherine and Mrs. Catlett were busy sweeping the parlor. Polly's bright hair was all pinned up under a cap. Her sleeves were rolled to the elbows, and her work apron brushed the floor.

"Polly," Johnny began, "I must leave right after dinner, around one o'clock, to catch the mail coach. I don't know when I'll be back. Polly, dear, say you will answer my letters."

Polly looked at him with that clear gaze he found so unnerving. Her dainty little hands formed and shaped the cookies. "Yes, I will answer," she said softly.

"Oh, Polly, Polly—."

She stopped him with a look, and he leaned against the table for a few minutes, watching the sugar fly as she sprinkled cookie dough. She knew very well how he felt. She knew, and she kept him in his place like a little woman. Not yet fourteen, and she could be serious, or she could be so gay, her bright laughter filling any room she was in.

"Another voyage might last two years, Polly. Two years before I see you again. If I could sign aboard a ship sailing to Africa, I'd be back within two years. Or maybe my father can find me a position in England, and I could visit you." He secretly doubted very much that his father could find him a land job. He was not suited for any work except that of sailor.

"Polly, if I ship outward bound again, will you sometimes look at the North Star at midnight, and I'll look at it, too, and I'll know you are looking at it—." He stopped, confused.

"I'm abed by nine o'clock," Polly said primly.

"Oh, of course, I didn't think. Will you look at the North Star at eight o'clock each night? Polly, Polly, dear!"

Again she checked him with a look, and he waited patiently. "Yes, sometimes I'll look," she said.

He couldn't bear to say good-bye after dining, but simply held out his big, rough hand. After hesitating, Polly lightly touched his hand and turned away.

Johnny bit his lips, hurried into his clothes in the hallway, feeling that his heart would surely break and he would fall down dead and then she would be sorry.

Mrs. Catlett hugged him and shut the hall door, so no one else would hear. "Johnny, we all love you. To me, you're like a son. Johnny, dear, I see how it is with you about my Polly, and you must not come here again unless she is away from the house."

Johnny fought to hold back tears he hadn't shed since he was a small child. "Johnny, don't be taking it amiss. She's a child. Some day I will be proud to see you ask for our Polly's hand. Someday when you have a good job and some prospects for the future. Before the good Lord took your ma we agreed on this. You do understand, don't you?"

Johnny felt torn between grief and fury. Yes, God took his mother away from him when he was only seven years old, so he hated God. Yes, he understood that there was no hope. He would never have "prospects" or captain a ship. He could see Polly wedded, bedded with a country lout with sheep manure on his hands!

He permitted Mrs. Catlett to kiss him on the cheek, then ran down the front steps, to the crossroads, and just caught the mail coach. He couldn't sleep. He slumped in one corner, beside two fat gentlemen. His love was a dark fire locked up in his chest until he almost wished he had never seen the girl.

Back in Liverpool, afraid to face his father, he walked the streets until dusk. The names of the ships that docked were posted on a sheet of paper on the side of a building near the waterfront. He stopped to read: *Hero, Prince of Wales, Fame, Harwich, Rainbow.* The ship for Jamaica was long gone.

Footsteps behind him in that lonely street made him swing around but the man—the men—sidestepped into an alley. Johnny's heart quickened in fear. *Steady,* he told himself. *Stay out in the open.* Walking briskly, he listened for the steps behind him. There must be three of them! If he ran now, he might outrun them. Wait! Two more men approached him, slowly, closing in.

Five of them! Now Johnny was sure who they were. In the dim light he saw dirty white trousers, dark blue coats, and cocked hats. A press gang from the Royal Navy! Looking to kidnap men and force them on to a man-of-war.

They'd never take him alive, Johnny vowed. He scooped up

a glass wine bottle from the gutter, cracked its neck, and held a jagged weapon. The moment they heard the glass break, the men rushed him. Three from behind tore his coat down the back, but he fought like a madman, slashing one of them and cutting his own hand. Blood flew everywhere as the two men in front clubbed him over the head.

Johnny lunged at them with the gory bottle and sliced a man's sleeve and into his arm. "I'll tear your tripes out!" he screamed. With a growl of rage, the tough grabbed Johnny's arm and twisted.

"Don't break no bones," warned the junior officer. "A heap of good he'd be without an arm. Come along, you devil. You're an able seaman, I can tell. No, we won't be letting the likes of *you* get away!"

Johnny bit and kicked, but he lost his weapon, and in a trice they had him trussed up like a pig and slung over the burly officer's shoulder.

"Curse you for murdering dogs, you—!"

"That'll do, ducky," said one man as they trotted along toward the ship. "Knock 'im on the head again, Billy."

Johnny felt another dull blow on the head. Just before he floated off into blackness, he saw a golden-haired girl with eyes like the sea. She slowly melted down, the way a wax candle does, and was gone forever.

4

Aboard a Man-of-war

Johnny woke up in the sick berth of the ship, doubled up in a hammock that bumped against a half-dozen other hammocks. About seventy men swung in hammocks, packed together like herring in a barrel, down in the depths of the ship. The ship's doctor, along with his mate, crawled under the hammocks, then squirmed upright to examine each man, banging their heads against the bodies.

"Son of a sea cook! What's this able-bodied man doing taking up room here?" The doctor's ruffled white shirt was blood-stained. His sleeves were rolled up tight, with dirt in the creases.

"Seems like his topsail is busted," the mate spoke cheerfully. "We'll splice 'im up, sir. He'll do jolly well in a day or two."

"He'll do jolly well right now!" the doctor snorted. "Has he pulses? Good. Then roll yourself out of there, you ruffian! Taking up space in His Majesty's sick berth, you young Turk! Report to the captain and sign in."

Johnny sat up, head swimming. A familiar face in the next

47

hammock. A familiar voice. "Mister Jewet, sir, I'll answer for him. His head was hurt bad, and his arm's twisted. His starboard eye is black as the coal pit, as you can see. You'll be letting him mend a little, sir? He's an able seaman, he is."

Steenie! Johnny eased over the hammock edge and flexed his battered legs. Slowly he forced himself to his feet.

"You're on no mollycoddling merchant ship now!" the doctor said, shoving angrily at the hammocks that bumped against him. "You're on board a man-o'-war in the Royal Navy. Look sharp! And you take notice, too, Mr. Handwick. You've got pulses? Then you ain't dead, so get up and walk!"

With this awful warning, the doctor wiped his hands on his wig, disappeared under the hammocks, and crawled away. His mate followed, dragging rags and a pail of water.

"We'd do better up where there's air," Steenie said. "The smells of this place give me fear in the bowels." Johnny dropped to his hands and knees. Together they crawled under the hammocks and made their way to the ladder. The sick men moaned and cried and called for water and light, and there was no one to help.

Up on deck, Johnny doused a bucket of water over his head and tidied himself as best he could. "How did they get you?"

"We was almost back to the *Dareway*. Captain Abell saw it all from the ship. The press-gang got nine of his crew."

"Ned—?"

"Right you are. Ned and Old Burgoo and Ralph, Willie, Sander, Dick, Chester, and one unbeknown to me. The ship's boat was clove hitched to the piling, and we were casting off when they pulled us right out."

"My head's stove in, I believe." Johnny sat down on a coil of rope and considered his fate. A man-of-war. For five years. There was no escape.

"French ships been sneaking around our shores," Steenie said. "There could be war—any day. We're on the H.M.S. *Harwich*, bound for the East Indies, part of a fleet of twenty ships. She's got seventy-four guns and two hundred men on board."

The third mate came by and ordered them to report to the purser for clothes and assignments. Johnny was allowed fifteen inches of hammock space and a small sea chest for his belongings. The fo'c'sle, in the bow of the ship, was a dark cave full of evil smells, lice, and bugs. Scummy water sloshed underfoot. Johnny stowed away his torn coat with his father's letter to Mr. Beekman, which would never be delivered now.

The following day Captain Drummond ordered all hands on deck, and the men were divided into able seamen, ordinary seamen, and landsmen. Able seamen went aloft to tighten or slacken the rigging. Ordinary seamen worked on deck, on the braces, sheets, brails, and halyard ropes. Landsmen ran errands, waited on officers, or manned the guns. Skilled men were called "idlers" because they did not have to take a turn at the watch. They worked hard at mending sails, carpenter work, blacksmith work, and painting the ship.

While the *Harwich* still lay at anchor, the captain ordered a drill. The drummer boy beat out an alarm. The bosun cried, "All hands!" and Johnny leaped up the rigging. In two minutes he was at his post on the lower topsail of the mizzenmast, flattening down the sail, making it tight.

Hundreds of men down on the main deck ran to their battle posts. On the gun decks, men sweated and cursed as they swung the big guns into position, ready to fire broadsides at the enemy.

A gun firing half-pound grapeshot was hauled up to the platform next to Johnny. "Here I stand, a fair target for any Frenchie musketeer," he muttered, looking around uneasily. Below, the captain, gorgeous in full dress and wig, paced the quarterdeck, timing the drill.

Afterward, Johnny found Steenie and Ned at mess and complained bitterly. "I shan't put up with this for long. The vittles are bad. No shore leave lest the men desert. All that gunpowder stored right beneath my hammock. I tell you, I'll slip over the side and swim for it!"

"Don't be rash, lad," Steenie said. "As Christian gentlemen we'll serve our king and—."

Johnny's temper boiled hot, and he snarled, "I serve no one but myself! So much for your God!" He spit on the deck and let fly a few of his favorite curses. His imagination came alive, and he added a few more he invented. Shock was stamped on the men's faces.

"Johnny, lad," Steenie protested, "don't be speaking such of the Almighty. Come, hold your tongue. Keep an even keel, lad. We'll manage."

Johnny felt himself go out of control, and he swung at the man nearest him, a man whose face he had never seen before.

"You cowardly skulk!" The sailor ducked Johnny's fists, tripped him neatly, and stepped aside as Johnny's head cracked the wooden floor. "Had enough, you dog? Do pardon me. Faith, 'twas an accident."

Steenie dragged him to his feet. "Do you want a flogging? Come below, lad, we'll talk about it."

Johnny allowed himself to be led back to his hammock. His head spun like a top, and Steenie had to hoist him into bed.

"Help me get a letter to my father," Johnny said, when he could talk. "He could get me transferred off here, had he a mind to. Captain Drummond may even know him. Ask the mate if I can see the captain, will you?"

"Not 'til I've patched you up a bit," Steenie said, rooting in Johnny's sea chest for cloth. "Ho, what's this? A letter. To a Mr. Beekman at Maidstone and from your father."

"That letter!" Johnny held out his hand. "That letter will prove who I am. Lock it up again, Steenie, lest these pick-pockets find it. I'll clean up and politely ask the captain to be put ashore or exchanged on to another ship."

"Ahoy! Ahoy!" A familiar bundle of rags skipped by, and Old Burgoo wagged his finger at Johnny. "Gut me if it ain't our Johnny, not geared right in his upper works! Has he pulses? Has he pulses?" His skinny fingers pinched Johnny's elbow. "Aye, fine pulses! Oh, our Johnny'll live to stand in the Judgment Day, he will! I swear by the parson's nose he'll live!"

"Back like a bad penny," Johnny snorted.

"A reg-lar basketful of words," Steenie said. "Burgoo, are ye ship's cook now?"

"Oh, dear me, no." Burgoo laid a finger alongside his nose. "Oh, do be mum. I never let on I'm a cook, oh, dear, no. They's three cooks already on this ship. I'm made assistant to the doctor, I am."

"Methinks he's slipped his cable," Steenie grunted.

"Allow me to check your pulses." Old Burgoo gave Steenie's arm a sharp tweak. "My good fellow, Old Burgoo stands by the doctor, ready to assist."

Johnny knew that grinning would only encourage him, so he didn't. "Assist in what?"

"Why, the bucket. I carries away the bucket of limbs when he chops 'em off. An easier life than trying to keep my feet in a slippery galley in a gale."

Ned came to offer his help in cleaning up Johnny. "You can borrow my suit and neckerchief if you're granted leave to speak to the captain."

Johnny thanked him. A few days' rest and time for his cut head to heal and he'd approach the captain.

When he did, he found Captain Drummond not at all a bad sort. In fact he already knew his father.

"Old Newton's son," he mused, looking at the letter. "Well, now, have you had schooling, sir? I can see you're no fresh-water mariner. Can you compute latitude and longitude and distance, without landmarks? Have you mastered your math and the Rutter?"

Johnny felt right at ease. He could recite the mariner's handbook of ancient lore regarding tides, compass bearings, and so forth. He proceeded to enlighten the captain. He knew he made a fine picture in Ned's brown suit and red neckerchief, Steenie's almost-new white stockings, his own boots. Chester, the barber, did good work on his beard and sideburns, pasting a lock of hair over the head wound.

Captain Drummond leaned back in his carved chair and fingered the compass. "Well, now. Old Newton's son, hmmmm? Suppose I make you midshipman, lad? Six years of service, then you'll be a lieutenant."

"Yessir, I'd do my duty, sir." Johnny thought of Polly and how she'd stare when she saw him promoted already. Now he'd have eight hours on duty, sixteen off. A good life.

"Present yourself to be fitted out with dress clothes and sword," the captain said. "I expect my men to look their best at all times and learn all they can." He dismissed Johnny with a wave of the hand, and Johnny hurried off to tell Steenie and Ned of his good fortune.

He certainly *meant* to turn over a new leaf, but every time he thought of five years without seeing Polly, he rebelled. The fleet still hadn't sailed, since the winter weather was bad, and the *Harwich* lay at anchor. One day Johnny hit upon a bold plan. He asked the first mate's permission to go ashore and say good-bye to the dear friend of the family who had nursed his mother when she lay dying of consumption. The mate asked the captain, and word came back that Midshipman John Newton was granted one day of shore leave.

Johnny went ashore in the ship's small boat, feeling ten years older, knowing he looked smart in his dress clothes and Ned's topcoat. Once again he caught the mail coach to Maidstone in Kent and knocked at the Catlett door.

Mrs. Catlett was astonished. "What, Johnny? Promoted already?" She seemed to forget she had forbidden him to return and made him feel at home. The next morning he and Polly were alone in the sitting room.

Polly smiled shyly this time, and Johnny talked freely, boasting of his position. "I must be gone tomorrow," he said. "The fleet sails for the East Indies to escort some merchant

ships back home and to patrol the waters. We expect war with
France. Marmalade Madame must be taught a lesson—that *we*
are master of the seas." He flushed, realizing he shouldn't have
used those words.

War. Did he imagine she looked worried? She was a sweetheart of a girl. He could see gold-dust specks in her eyes when
she looked at him. And the glorious flood of hair falling down
like a gold cape. She was so dainty-small in her long, brown
wool dress, so pert and watchful. Johnny felt his heart sicken
with love. If he could only get a promise from her that she
would wait for him.

"What have you been reading?" he asked.

"Oh, poetry," she said softly. "Stories written for young
ladies. My prayer book and the Bible."

"Poetry? Do you like Shakespeare's sonnets?"

"Oh, yes. I like 'Shall I compare thee to a summer's day?' "

" '... Thou art more lovely and more temperate,' " Johnny
finished. "Very appropriate."

She flushed and looked down. "And I like, 'Poor soul, the
centre of my sinful earth.' And *MacBeth* and the shorter plays,
though Mother has to explain many of the words."

"Thine eyes I love," thought Johnny, but he wisely kept it to
himself. Other lines ran silently through his head. *"How like
a winter hath my absence been From thee, the pleasure of the
fleeting year! What freezings have I felt, what dark days seen!"*
Outloud he said, "Polly, I may be gone six years or more."

She extra carefully tied a triple knot in her embroidery work
before she looked up. Her hoop held a white handkerchief
edged in lace. She was decorating it with colored threads, a design of knife, fork, and a little pink spoon.

"We had the nicest snow frolic, Catherine and I," she said
gaily. "The Broden girls came over to play, then Mother gave
us all hot chocolate and the bread I baked, fresh from the oven.
I'm learning to play the flute, too. Winter evenings are so
long."

"Polly Catlett—Polly Newton," Johnny said softly, one ear

listening for her mother in the next room. He reached out to touch her needlework. "I can use a pretty handkerchief like that at sea." He *must* have something of hers to take with him.

She flashed him a startled look. " 'Tis meant for a lady."

"Polly, please." He gently took the hoop, slipped it open, and tucked the morsel of cloth in Ned's coat pocket. "Polly, it's all I'll have—." He almost choked on the words, remembering.

She stood up, frightened, knocking over her small rocking chair. At the noise Mrs. Catlett hurried into the room, alarmed and frowning.

"I—I was saying good-bye," Johnny stammered. "I have just one day of leave. I've overstayed. I thank you kindly, ma'am, and I really must catch the mail coach today." He cursed his voice for cracking like an awkward schoolboy's and held out his hand. "Good-bye, Polly."

As before, she touched his hand briefly and turned away.

In the hall, Mrs. Catlett helped him on with his topcoat. "Johnny, I must remind you of your promise. Polly is a child. Someday, Johnny."

Johnny let himself be kissed, then ran down the steps. Six years! No, he wouldn't stand it! There must be a way! He'd do anything for her, work hard, die for her. As he waited in the snow, stamping his feet to keep warm, it occurred to him: He had never before loved an *innocent* girl.

Back on shipboard, Mr. Learner, the third mate, sent for him. He was a tall, lean man, fortyish, a voice like the bite of lemon. "Captain's compliments, he began sarcastically, "and he wishes to say he takes notice you overstayed your leave."

"I am truly sorry," Johnny said promptly. "My dear family friend took a chill and fell most dreadfully ill, and there was no one there, sir, save ourselves and the cook, sir. I helped keep the coals hot in the bedwarming pan that kept her from an even worse chill, sir, and I'm sorry, sir, and kindly begging the captain's pardon."

Mr. Learner arched his thin eyebrows and pursed his lips. "Forgiven this time, Mr. Newton. That's all."

Johnny turned to go, then stopped. "Mr. Learner, sir, might I teach my friend, Ned Meadows, some of the Rutter and such? He'd make a mighty good officer. Was a master in a boys' school, sir, a highly intelligent fellow."

Mr. Learner surprised him. "Mr. Newton, it will put your mind at ease to know we have our eye on young Meadows and Ralph Beckett and a few others for promotion in the Royal Navy. It is highly possible you can work together."

Ralph! Johnny hid his annoyance. *That white-livered, mush-mouthed lubber. Bookish and fine talking, but a mean beast.*

Johnny was quartered now with the other midshipmen, so he moved his hammock and sea chest near Ned and Chester in the deckhouse. Chester had been midshipman on the *Mermaid*, an Indiaman, so he was experienced. Red-haired, quiet, no-nonsense he was, and Johnny thought he'd like him.

Two nights before the fleet sailed, the captain allowed some skylarking. Boatloads of girls, fiddlers, gamblers, and fortune-tellers were rowed out to the ship. Peddler women, from bum-boats, were welcomed on board to sell their merchandise.

Party time on the huge main deck! Sailors all in fresh cottony britches, long-sleeved striped shirts, and peaked caps began to skip and dance and jig. The fiddlers sawed on the strings with all their might. From overhead a lantern swung and smoked its dim light on to the faces of men reading last letters from home.

Old Burgoo, his bare knees knocking, his little monkey face aflame with liquor, pranced and danced and made rhymes for his audience.

> "A hey nonnie-no, all lubbers be drowned!
> Burgoo's in the stew, and we're outward bound.
> The stew's in burgoo, come laddies, treat 'im nice,
> This ship won't come back till h__ freezes ice!"

"More rum for Old Burgoo!" The men cheered and passed glasses around and opened another keg.

Johnny sat apart with Ned, watching the fun. "Have a

drop?" a sailor next to them offered. Johnny shook his head.
"Not now." He hadn't the heart for anything, knowing this
noisy hole would be his home for five years. And Polly?

Such a longing swept over him that he thought he would go
mad. *Polly, Polly, Polly.* Every night he had dreamed of her.
Every waking moment was filled with her. He saw those eyes,
holding his gaze, then her cheeks flooded with sudden color.
He saw her white, dimpled arms lifted to hang a towel to dry
over the kitchen fire. And her hair! Curled around her face,
hanging in waves to her waist. All the shades of gold in the
world. Her little, slippered feet and fuzzy pink wool stockings.

In her presence he'd felt like a better person. With her at his
side, he could change his ways. Why, she would be twenty
years old before they'd meet again! A little beauty like Polly
would not stay single long.

"What's the trouble?" Ned shook his arm and looked into
his face. "Why are you groaning? Your old wound hurt?"

Yes, the old wound hurt. "I think I'll go below," he said.

A pretty chippy danced up to him and tried to sit in his lap.
"Take a turn with me, dearie, that's a brave lad."

"Go along with you." He gave her a shove.

She pouted, then attached herself to Ned. "And will *you*
dance, sir? A poor sailor needs a little fun before he ships hisself out."

"I don't mind," Ned said, taking her arm. "Just to dance,
you understand."

She giggled up into his face. "Ah, sir, you must oblige me.
How's a poor, pretty orphan girl to live?"

They danced away, and Johnny saw her cleverly slip her fingers into the pockets of Ned's brown coat, searching for money
or anything to steal. After a while the fiddlers fell silent to wipe
their faces and have another drink.

There was a little scream from the black-eyed chippy dancing with Ned. She pulled out a dainty white handkerchief from
his pocket, embroidered with a little pink knife, fork, and
spoon.

"Oh, me!" she pretended to feel faint. "I am betrayed! He has another!"

Polly's handkerchief. Johnny ground his teeth and was on his feet in a second. *Hold! I can't let them know. Don't show any feeling.* He'd forgotten Ned was again wearing the brown suit he'd lent to him.

Ned looked his surprise, then glanced around for Johnny. He understood. Ralph, idling on a bench saw the look. Now *he* knew.

"Oh, me!" shrieked the giddy girl. "A sweetheart! Do tell, is she fair? Has she eyes of blue? Hair like gold? Did she swear to be true and never look at another?"

A sailor snatched the handkerchief, and the men passed it around, sniffing its perfume, laughing, making crude remarks. Ned laughed in good nature and held his tongue. They teased him without mercy.

Ralph sat smiling to himself as though he were making some pleasant plans for the future.

One of the drunken men blew his nose on the precious bit of fluff, and Johnny had to stand and watch and do nothing. Ralph laughed to himself until his shoulders wobbled, turning his flat head now and then to enjoy Johnny's suffering.

By now the men had torn the handkerchief to bits, fighting over it and roaring their pleasure. The bold chippy ripped the sleeve off her red blouse and threw it to the men. "And wouldn't ye fight over me?" she cried. The drunken men crowded around her, and she threw them her scarf, her apron, one stocking.

Johnny turned from the scene and headed wildly for his quarters. His vision of Polly, his hope, his dreams were all dead. He'd be better dead, he thought, than alive in such pain. He'd be better dead.

5

Deserter!

The H.M.S. *Harwich* sailed from Spithead with a very large fleet. Early in the morning Johnny dressed and followed Mr. Hopkins, lieutenant. "Stay by me," the officer said. "You'll learn as you go."

On the quarterdeck Mr. Hopkins shouted the captain's orders through his speaking trumpet as the topmen climbed aloft. Bells clanged, chains jangled. Sails and rigging were handled in perfect teamwork.

"Brace the yards!" Mr. Hopkins hollered.

The riggers hauled on the ropes, straining, bracing feet, making the rope fast to an iron belaying pin along the ship's rail. Each sail represented tons of force, almost pulling arms out of sockets.

Mr. Hopkins ordered a man to pull in a brace on the leeward side. "Hold! Haul again!"

Johnny watched a sight he had seen thousands of times before. Already he felt he could handle the job.

"Lay aloft and loose the fore lower topsail! Man the fore lower topsail sheets!"

The captain paced the deck, nodded to the first mate. "Up anchor!"

The sails began to shiver as the wind touched them. "Turn her to leeward!" the captain shouted to the helmsman. "Now bring her up to windward!"

The *Harwich* moved with the tide, part of a fleet of beautiful white-winged birds. The man sounding the depth called out his findings every so often. Johnny gazed at England's shore slipping away from him. All he felt was the blackest despair at leaving Polly.

No one expected the wind to turn so suddenly, but it came against them, a storm broke, and the fleet put into Torbay for the night. The next day was fair, but toward nightfall the fleet passed the coast of Cornwall, and a storm from the south fought against them.

"Came so sudden the captain says the ship is jinxed," Mr. Hopkins told them. "Give a hand with the rigging, Johnny. Some of the casks broke loose, and the third mate crushed his leg. Tried to get up on deck and got washed back down with a barrel atop him."

Aye, midshipman, just too good a job to last, Johnny thought bitterly, climbing the ratlines in the sheeting rain. The night was dark as a beggar's pocket, and the ship reeled from side to side.

He knew the danger of her crashing into other ships and being wrecked right within sight of England. Below, the suck and pull of rushing foam loosened more barrels, and he saw men crawling across the deck and strangled by the wash of waves.

The ship was wrung like a rag, swabbed about in crazy circles, wrung again, and brutally thrown over to starboard, almost sinking out of sight. The whole world reeled. They had been caught with sails set, and now it was almost too late to furl them.

Along with four other men, Johnny lay on the freezing canvas, trying to smother it, blowing on his frozen fingers. His cap blew away, and he shuddered hard in the squally wind. Working from lee to weather side, the five of them managed to furl the sail.

The hammering of wind against his mouth forbade any talk with the other men. One by one they backed down the ratlines in the dark, onto the slimy planks of the deck.

As Johnny held a lifeline and began to pull hand over hand to get below, he was knocked to his knees with the force of the explosion of a ship on their starboard side. Billows of flame and smoke lit the sky. The waist of the doomed ship dipped down; then the bow and stern shot up into the air and, like a fan folded, the ship sank.

Their powder magazine, Johnny thought, struggling to his feet. His legs washed out from under him, and a wave slapped his face and whooshed in his mouth, nearly gagging him.

Another ship foundered on the rocks, and he was terrified by the grinding and splintering he heard over the snapping fangs of the wind. He bumped into a warm body and saw a face with furry eyebrows and a head tied with a long rag. "Johnny?"

It was Steenie. They swayed together on the rope. "Mate says all get below, or we're lost!" he shouted into Johnny's ear. "He tried to anchor, the anchor slipped 'er cable, and we'll see England again by the grace of God! The *Fame*—she's bearing down on us in the dark—can't get a glim aloft—we're bein' run down by our own fleet! Get below!"

"What ship sank?"

"The *Admiral!*"

The *Harwich* was one big sloshing earthquake. Hand over hand Johnny followed Steenie, who turned around once more. He put his mouth to Johnny's ear. "Pray!" he screeched. "Pray! Pray!"

Somewhere a cracked yardarm banged against the mast. Pray? Johnny had never prayed in his life. Even should there be a God, it wasn't likely He'd give ear to Johnny Newton. There wasn't a ray of hope for Johnny Newton with the Almighty.

Then how could he explain the words that flashed into his mind—words from childhood and a gentle mother's face he saw again though the storm still raged and blew: "Wages of sin ... death ... gift of God ... eternal life. ..."

No, not for him. He'd tried many a time to improve and mend his ways, and it didn't work. Bible stories were for babes. Death ended everything.

He and Steenie dropped safely below deck and waited out the rest of the awful night. Morning found the fleet at Plymouth, laid up for repairs. The captain sent a small boat ashore, and when it returned, Johnny heard the news that his father had come down to Torbay on business. If he could only speak to him and plead once again for help in getting off the *Harwich* and onto a ship in the African trade. He would be back to England within two years. He didn't give a farthing for being a midshipman on a man-of-war.

"Don't do it, Johnny," Steenie advised. "Bad luck follows you like a pig follows corn. Have you heard the sad news? Old Burgoo washed right off the deck and seen no more." Steenie sniffled and blew his nose hard. "We'll never see another like Burgoo. Blamed hard on a man."

Johnny felt only a slight pang. All his thoughts centered on quitting the ship at the first opportunity. The *Harwich* would be laid up two weeks at least. Finally his chance came when Mr. Hopkins asked him to go ashore with ten men, to see they didn't desert. "Men are restless, talking of bad luck aboard," the officer said. "Take them ashore for some fun, but be back by dark, mind. Each day we'll send a few ashore to post their letters and visit around."

Johnny washed his clothes as best he could and put them under Ned's mattress to smooth them. The next morning he lowered himself into the jolly boat and went ashore with the men. He wore a sword and pistol in his belt, and his cocked hat showed him to be a member of the Royal Navy. Surely his father would be impressed and would forgive him and help him again.

He settled the men in a cheap alehouse, ordered a round of drinks, and told them to wait until he posted a letter. Ducking out the back door of the tavern, he walked fast, keeping an eye out for anyone from the fleet. He had some knowledge of the roads, and by guessing his way at each crossroads, he headed toward Dartmouth. That night he slept in a barn, curled up next to the cow, under a layer of hay.

In the morning he forced himself to eat two raw eggs found alongside a hen, then walked briskly toward Torbay. Within two hours, he would be there and under his father's protection.

As he rounded a bend in the road five soldiers caught sight of him. "Halt! Throw down your arms, sir!" Johnny obliged, cursing the luck.

"How are you so far from your ship, sir?" The leader circled him, taking note of the cut of his clothes. Johnny didn't answer.

"We're sent to find one John Newton, deserter from His Majesty's ship *Harwich*," the soldier said. "We're sent to find one who let ten other seamen escape His Majesty's service. One who was trusted by his captain and who broke that trust. Give account of yourself, sir."

Johnny didn't answer but gnawed his lip and stared at the ground. Two more hours and he'd have been safe.

"I see we've caught our bird in the snare," the soldier said, roping Johnny's arms behind him. "Now march, sir, back to your ship and the reward that waits for you."

The leader walked ahead, and the other men marched two on each side of him. So he returned to Plymouth guarded like a low-down criminal. He was marched through the streets for the amusement of the people who had nothing else to laugh at, then sent out to the *Harwich*, still bound and guarded.

The first mate welcomed him with curses, blows, and vile words. "You traitor to the king! You woodenhead! You clod of mud! Blood, but you deserve to swing for this! 'Twould pleasure me to kill you! Ten able-bodied men gone! Aye, you'll have your reward! Throw him in irons!"

Two sailors dragged him across the deck, where he was chained in leg irons on the top gun deck and lay for two days and nights in the weather, without food or drink. No man dared go near him.

Johnny was half-dead with fear and shame. The third morning, at eleven o'clock, the bosun piped all hands on deck for the flogging. Captain Drummond and the officers wore their best, swords by their sides. Johnny, hands tied together, was hauled upright, to the rolling beat of a drum. A burly sailor dragged him before the captain.

"John Newton, have you anything to say for yourself?"

Johnny didn't answer.

"Strip!"

With his knife a sailor neatly nipped up the neck of Johnny's shirt and slit it down the back.

Captain Drummond's face was hard as iron, and he showed no mercy. "Seize him up!"

The mate tied Johnny's hands to an overhead spar. "Seized up, sir," he reported.

"Uncover your heads." The men obeyed respectfully.

The captain opened a book and read from the Articles of War: " 'Whereas you, John Newton, have knowingly and willfully deserted ship during threat of war, also taking with you ten able seamen and instructing them likewise to desert, His Gracious Majesty under God doth sentence you to fifty lashes. Furthermore, you shall be demoted to the rank of ordinary seaman. Bosun mate, do your duty."

Johnny squeezed his eyes shut, breathing, "Polly . . . , Polly . . . ," but his voice wasn't heard as the mate slashed down the cat-o-nine-tails whip with all his might.

"Uhhhhhh," Johnny moaned under his breath, feeling a streak of fire on his bare back. They wouldn't hear him cry— never! The next two lashes cut deeper, and blood ran down the back of his legs. Then shock after shock until there was nothing left in the world but pain.

The bosun mate tired, and another mate stepped up. Drawing a deep breath, he swung the knotted ropes down on Johnny's back. Blood splattered on the man nearby. Johnny felt a scream begin in his brain, but he turned his mouth to his shoulder and bit into it.

Now his stockings and shoes were soaked in blood, and he began to sway from side to side. The blood thudding in his ears made him blind and dizzy. When the count was only at thirty-two he fainted.

He woke up, wishing he had died. He was back in the fo'c'sle, lying on his side in a hammock. His agony was so great he would have thrown himself over the side of the ship, had he been able to walk. The men were forbidden to speak to him or assist him in any way.

Only Steenie, after mess at nighttime, brought him a little water and a biscuit. Johnny shook his head, eyes closed. "Stow it under yer shirt," Steenie said. "You'll need it later. Precious mad the captain was, Johnny, for wot you did. The old croak swears you will never be promoted now. Says he'll learn you to be law abiding." Steenie choked up as he patted Johnny's matted hair. "What a sight you are! Your back hangs in a million pieces, all pulp and ribbons."

Johnny moaned and tried to throw up, but there was nothing in his stomach.

"Johnny, Johnny, why do ye do such things?" Steenie crooned on. "Johnny, when you're healed up, can't we two sit down and talk about God and His love and how He'll help you, lad, if you only seek Him and be guided by the Book?"

Johnny tossed his head from side to side in fever. "Get oil for my back," he groaned.

"I darsen't be seen talkin' to you, lad, or helpin' you. But I'll try. The doctor ain't all that stonyhearted. Keep your courage, lad. If only Old Burgoo could be with us, he'd stand true to you. First him ... then you a-dyin'...." Steenie sobbed into his hands.

"You crazy old loon!" Johnny spoke without opening his eyes. "Swipe me some laudanum or opium for the pain. I'll show him I'll not die. I'll live to kill him, I will. I swear it."

Steenie jerked his head up, his eyes wet and smeary. "By all that's sacred you are a rough one! Aye, I'll fetch you oil, else you'll die of a hard heart!"

When he returned, the other men were asleep, and Johnny felt him slip three small bottles into his hand. "Old Bones was right good about it, and, 'Keep it from the captain,' he says. Take one small sip of each every time you hear the watch sing out, and you'll be eased."

Johnny waited until Steenie had climbed into his hammock, then he drank the contents of all three bottles and fell into a stupor. He knew nothing for two days and two nights. When he woke up, some of the pain was gone, and he was hungry.

He was able to stand in line for mess, and in two more days he could put his shirt on without wanting to scream. He was ignored by the officers who used to like him. As he swabbed down the deck and holystoned it with the little square blocks of sandstone resembling prayer books, he could look up and see Ned and Ralph on the quarterdeck. Ned raised his eyebrows by way of greeting, but he didn't dare take any further notice. Ralph smiled widely and often leaned down to watch Johnny slave away. But it was a smile of triumph and glee at his suffering.

The fleet sailed, and all chance of escape was cut off. Johnny was given the hardest jobs, the jobs no one else wanted. He emptied the slops from the toilets and scrubbed them out on his hands and knees. He was sent aloft whenever it was most dangerous and slippery. All the time he was planning how to be revenged upon the captain. Not once did it ever occur to him that he himself was to blame for any of his troubles.

He thought of simply bursting into Captain Drummond's cabin, grabbing the captain's pistol, and shooting him in the chest. But then he would be hung, and Polly would know. He thought of poison in the captain's food. Where could he obtain poison? He thought of an accident in the dark during a storm.

He remembered the three glass bottles the ship's doctor had

sent him. Ground into powder, the glass could be mixed with food.

One afternoon, when he had time off and the other men were lazing around reading and writing letters, Johnny opened his sea chest and broke the three medicine bottles. Keeping his head bent down in the chest, he worked quietly, grinding the broken glass between two blocks of wood.

"Keeping warm in there?" a man joked, stopping to look. The first time anybody bothered to speak to him since his flogging.

"Aye, cleaning the closet out," Johnny said, dropping some socks over the glass.

The man left, and Johnny figured it out as he worked. Sunday evening the captain would read prayers, then order an extra ration of grog for the men. The captain would then retire to his own cabin to dine on fresh-killed lamb, roasted brown, and vegetables. Certainly there would be wine first, and he'd be relaxed and off guard.

If he could get into the kitchen at that moment when the captain's tray was made ready, he could do it. He'd never be caught. No friend of his would be blamed. Old Burgoo was dead, and Johnny didn't care tuppence about the new cooks.

Johnny scraped all the ground glass into a fourth bottle, locked the chest, and wore the key around his neck as did all the other fellows.

Sunday was clear but bitterly cold. The men lined up on the decks, shivering in their cotton pants and canvas jackets, while the captain read a long Psalm, then a page explaining the Psalm, then read a long prayer ending: "Gracious Father God Almighty, maker of heaven and earth and ruler of these seas, now grant protection to Your navy and protect our shores and those left behind as we set out on Thy business in the deep waters. Sustain and keep and comfort the men who serve Thee and Thy humble servant over this great ship and fleet."

Thus comforted, the thin, hungry men were dismissed. A few lucky ones huddled around the blacksmith's forge, another

dozen in the galley and mess, where there was heat, but the rest
of the six hundred kept warm in their imaginations.

Around suppertime Johnny presented himself to the cook, in
the galley, the bottle of ground glass underneath his shirt. The
cook—old Short Rations or Mr. Greening—tended six or
seven pots and pans on the iron stove. The ship was rolling a
little, and the pots bumped against the two-inch-high railing
on the stove top, but didn't fly off as they sometimes did.

"What d'ye want, Newton?" The cook was short and fat,
with a lame knee. His pulpy face was ruddy from leaning over
the hot stove and fleshy from tasting everything and helping
himself to meat on the sly.

"Compliments, Mr. Greening," Johnny said humbly, even
bobbing his head a little. "I'm sent to wash up the floor, sir, or
clean up, or help you in any way you see fit."

"Whose compliments d'ye say?"

"Mr. Lenn, sir," Johnny mumbled a name he had made up.
"The new gentleman, sir."

The cook scowled and stirred and licked the big wooden
spoon, stuck it into all the pots, stirred, and licked again. He
smacked his fat lips and opened the oven door a crack. The
delicious smells made Johnny's head swim and his mouth fill
with water. He could have cheerfully murdered the cook just to
get his hands on the food.

"Take the bucket o' peelings to the animals."

Johnny lifted the enamel pot full of garbage and started
away. When he was out of the cook's sight, he greedily ate all
he could hold of the vegetable peelings and scrapings, plus
some of the orange rinds. Down at the bottom of the pot he
found some curly gristle from meat and thought it the best
treat he ever ate. He sucked the last juice from the orange skins
and tasted cinnamon on one. Gad! What a feast!

He emptied the bucket of slops to the sheep and chickens
below, and obediently returned to the galley. Short Rations
was preparing the captain's tray: slabs of roast lamb, oozing in

gravy; potatoes; turnips; fresh-baked bread; and a great dish of pudding.

Ah! The pudding! After the captain ate all that food and had a few glasses of wine, he'd scarcely notice what was in the pudding.

Short Rations stirred and tasted and put a dollop of pudding on a cracked saucer. "Here, take a bit."

"My thanks." Johnny ate with his fingers, very much surprised. The cook was a good lot. He'd be blamed, naturally, as no one knew Johnny was in the galley on a Sunday afternoon. Johnny licked the dish and handed it back, and the cook wiped it with a dirty rag and put it with the clean dishes.

"Mind the soup, will ye? Stir so's it don't stick to the bottom." The cook handed him a spoon and waddled into the next room. Quick as a thief Johnny uncorked his bottle, poured the ground glass into the pudding, stirred and fluffed it around, and turned back to watching the soup.

So easily done! When Short Rations returned, Johnny was busily stirring and tasting, stirring and tasting as he had seen the cook do. The soup was right savory!

"Here, boy." The cook gave him three onions and a burned biscuit. "Keep stirring. I'm running a little late, and the captain is hungry."

The steward arrived to carry the heavy tray to the captain's table, then he was gone. How easy! Johnny stirred and licked, enjoying himself.

In five minutes Short Rations was back, carrying the dish of pudding. "Steward reports the captain's stomach ain't right for a sweet. Here, lad, take it. You had a bad lashing, you did. Take the pudding and welcome."

Johnny's mouth fell open, but he took the dish. The cook stuck a rusty spoon in his hand. "Go ahead, lad, nobody'll know. Be quick, now."

"N-no, I can't." Johnny's hand shook. "I mean, I want to share it with the others—with Steenie—and—what's his name—."

"Yer a good lad," said the cook. "Go 'long, then, but bring the dish back, hear?"

Johnny nodded dumbly and hurried on deck. Sails furled for the night, the ship barely moved, and all was quiet. He heaved the dish overboard, then leaned his elbows on the bulwark railing, and his head felt heavy as iron in his hands. Only the thought of Polly kept him from slipping over the side to a cold, watery death.

6

The Midnight Rainbow

The closer the ship came to the Island of Madeira, the higher rose the spirits of the crew. The weather grew balmy and the sea even. Word spread that Captain Drummond would allow them all shore leave in relays. The ship would take on fresh water, the famous wines of Madeira, sugar, and honey for the captain's table.

The captain had relaxed his strictness with Johnny, though he never spoke to him again. The other sailors were friendlier to him, and he was again sent aloft, since he was a good worker. Many fine days he spent in the crow's nest, pipe in mouth, telescope in hand, an open book in his lap.

Johnny was loafing on deck during his four hours off duty one day when Ned approached. It was the first they were able to speak together since the flogging.

Some of the men were working on torn sails, some splicing ropes, and others plugging cracks in the deck with tar. Johnny smiled and patted his shirt, where a book was hidden inside. "Guess what I have been reading."

"*Rhapsody*," Ned replied promptly.

"Right you are." Johnny moved to make room for Ned. "Sit a spell. Nice to see you, Ned. I haven't found anybody else who reads books. This Lord Shaftesbury is a fine chap. I believe I have him all figured out now."

An old sailor with a massive, wobbly head like a barrel joined them. Red and white striped stockings drooped down over his pumps, and he wore a shawl draped around his middle. Twice he'd shipped out to the South Sea Islands, and the men called him Turtle Soup.

"I've had time to think," Johnny went on. "I've made a parcel of mistakes, as you know, but now I see religion is a good thing. This book says it is a discipline and a way to be perfect. Our own reason can help us avoid faults."

"Aye, right you are," Ned agreed. "There's nothing higher than yourself, you see. You must believe in yourself. Do whatever is good for you."

"Aye, religion is a most int'restin' thing," Turtle Soup broke into the conversation. "I mind how I seen two heathen a-cookin' of a missionary in a pot over a brave fire. 'Twas for his own good, I do believe. He gained heaven by it."

"Nonsense, my good man." Ned was annoyed. "Heaven is right here and now. Don't you be feeding us your silly yarns."

"It's only right there should be reward and punishment," Johnny went on, opening the small book. "How would the world fare without it?"

"But don't you see, reward and punishment is just for a time. Just while a man is a brute. However, as he grows up love will guide him." Ned turned the pages and pointed to a paragraph.

"Aye, love will guide him," said Turtle Soup dreamily. "I mind how the women would meet the ship in the islands, and a man could have his pick. Why they thought nothin' of—."

Ned cast him a dark look. "Do read the book before you speak, man. Perhaps then we could hold conversation."

"Can't read. Goes agin my religion."

Johnny laughed. "Turtle Soup, you poor turnip head! Listen to us, and you'll become educated." He turned back to Ned.

"Yes, I allow I've felt better about myself since I studied this book. Ned, I'm remembering so many things my mother taught me from the Bible."

"Your *mother?*" Ned sneered politely. "Then you have only inherited your mother's religion. You haven't yet formed ideas of your own."

Johnny looked at him in confusion. "I haven't inherited anything of the sort. I certainly do have my own ideas. You spoke highly of the Bible once."

"For me," said Turtle Soup strongly, "I'm an a-the-ist. It's a fine religion. Don't think it's easy to be an a-the-ist. Oh, no, it takes the greatest of faith." He looked down his nose at them as he braided his long black hair and tarred it.

"Do keep quiet, you shining example of a ninny!" Ned cried impatiently. "What I mean, Johnny, is that the Good Book was all right for *those* people thousands of years ago, unlearned and simple. Such an old Book cannot possibly help us today."

"But the miracles? Don't they prove the Bible true?"

"Miracles are no proof of anything. Suppose there *was* a miracle—what does it prove? Is it a good or bad power? Mortal or no? Wise or foolish? A just or unjust power? Still, it would be a mystery."

"A mystery to *me* how you go on so without wettin' your whistle with a drop of grog," Turtle Soup grumbled.

"There is not one speck of evidence for a divine being," Ned continued. "Nature is divine. Reason is divine. You have something divine in you. And in me. And in—," here he looked sideways at the old sailor. ". . . And even in *him!*"

Turtle Soup squirmed so his back was toward Ned. "I cannot abide that fellow," he said loudly. "He's got the nose drip!"

Johnny threw back his head and laughed. Becoming serious again, he said, "Ned, is all that in *Rhapsody?* Did I misunderstand it so much? How is a man to be good? For surely that is what we must try for?"

"All good is merely as we fancy it," Ned explained. "Suppose a man sets fire to a beautiful temple in order that people may remember his name after death? If this was the man's good, should we wonder at it?"

"Iffen I fired the ship some dark night," said Turtle Soup, "would you be remembering—?"

"Look here." Ned shoved the old man from between them. "You enjoy math and are good at it. Who is better able to do sums and figure out answers—the one who practices math or the one who is unlearned?"

"The one who works at math," Johnny agreed.

"So it is in life. Who is the best judge of living? The one who has really lived? Or the one who only talks about life?"

"The one who has really lived," said Johnny slowly.

"You see?" Ned said in triumph. "Lord Shaftesbury is saying all this in his book. Suppose you were attracted to the beauty of the ocean—."

"Ha!" snorted Turtle Soup. "The beauty of the ocean! The beauty of life at sea! The beauty of His Majesty's service! The beauty of burned biscuits and rumbly stommicks and dirty water! The beauty—."

"Do be quiet, or I shall throw you overboard." Ned glared at him. "Now suppose you were attracted to the beauty of the ocean, what would be the next thought?"

"To hire a ship and go out and wed myself to the sea," Johnny said.

"Exactly right."

Turtle Soup leered off into the distance. "And if you see beautiful women, how do you know what is good for you unless you try them all?"

Johnny didn't reply at once. Perhaps he *had* misunderstood the book. Ned was a schoolmaster and older than himself. But he still remembered his mother, a gentle soul, patient and sweet, and he still heard words of the Bible that used to calm him and make him want to be better. Words that rang true.

"Suppose you see a beautiful garden full of fruit," Ned went on. "How do you know what is good for you, unless you try them all?"

"What are you saying?"

"I am saying that we are masters of our lives, but we cannot decide about life until we have experienced everything good *and* bad. Each one must figure out what he needs to make him happy—then go after it!"

"I just needs a pipe at night, a wee mite more grog than I get, a chicken soup, thickishlike, an old woman to take care of me when I'm feeble, a nice island in the sun—."

"Shall I base my life on this book—*Rhapsody?*"

"No, no, the book just starts you thinking. Base your life on naught but yourself, Johnny."

"And Holy Scriptures?"

"Scripture is only a collection of religious tracts written by men like you and me. How did they know which ones to save and which to ignore? How do you know they were translated correctly?"

Johnny sighed. Ned made sense, he was so logical, he spoke from experience. A man could never reach up to God on his own. God—if there was a God—must be holy and mighty and powerful. What else was there to do but work out your own life? For him, all hope was gone of ever returning to England a rich man. Maybe he'd never live to see England again. Who knows where Polly would be six years from now?

The man on watch aloft cried out, "Land ho!" and excitement ran through the ship like a plague. Captain Drummond ordered extra grog, and the cook rolled out a keg. The mates tapped it and passed the drink around.

Turtle Soup hung over the railing. "The island! The island! Fish and flowers, grapes and garlic! Ow, *smell* the island! M'nose has landed already!"

It wasn't until the following day Johnny could actually smell the island: a warm, sweet, flowery smell.

"Taste the sun!" Turtle Soup lifted both arms in worship. "Paradise!"

Johnny saw tall, broken, rocky cliffs rising into the clouds, spreading out to sea and washed by glittering spray. The rocks formed natural arches. Rainbows hung all around them. He thought of half-sunken cathedrals with towers and peaks rising from the sea. A fresh breeze carried the village sounds aboard.

Ships of all nations anchored in Funchal, capital of the island of Madeira.

Johnny was among the first lot of men to go ashore for a day. The ship's small boat was not suitable because the beach was made of treacherous, loose, rolling gravel, so the land people sent out a strong boat. It had a high-peaked prow and stern to ride the heavy surf. The men crowded into the boat and waited. The men on land held a heavy rope attached to the boat.

"Here she comes!" sang out a sailor, and a high swelling wave lifted them up. The men on shore pulled on the rope with all their strength, and the boat crashed onto the beach and slid across the loose stones.

Johnny waded ashore and was surrounded by a dozen little beggar boys. *"Vosci bora.* Go away," he said, and they charged up to the next sailor. The officers back on the *Harwich* threw pennies over the side of the ship, and small boys dove into the clear water for them.

The port of Funchal was full of Spanish-type houses and vineyards grouped around the harbor. Johnny saw flower gardens, smelled strawberries and oranges and lemons and limes. Coffee plantations, bananas, waterfalls, deep blue sky with never a cloud. Turtle Soup was right—here was a paradise.

The captain was getting rid of several tons of unneeded ballast. Large boats, each with a rope attached, went out to the ship, were loaded, then hauled in by a capstan worked by bulls turning it around and around. The water was full of naked people working on boats, nets, fishing, and swimming.

Ned's bare feet twish-twished through the sand, and he rolled up his sleeves to get the sun. "It *is* a paradise, is it not? We can sleep right under a tree, unless. . . ." He jerked his shoulder to shore where a cluster of women waited, glossy black hair hanging below their shoulders, tanned to a buttery brown.

"That one's a dirty Sal—look at her arms," Ned pointed. "Now that one—I like her fore'n'aft." He winked.

The prettiest girl walked toward them. She wore a red and yellow dress and was barefooted.

"Why not?" said Ned. He took her hand and started off, calling back over his shoulder. "Pick one out, Johnny, and go home with her."

The warmth, the odors, the water music of the falls all made Johnny's head swim. After England and winter and all his suffering, he did indeed feel he was in paradise. A beauty with black-enamel flower-eyes came up to him and wordlessly put her arms around him. The sun stabbed his eyes, white-hot, and he felt good all over. Surely this was what life was all about. Slowly he took her hand, and they walked toward a little house with a low gateway leading into a big yard.

He spoke and understood her language, and she said her name was Resa, that her father was a trader but not at home. She earned extra money for them by "entertaining" sailors. She made it sound natural and innocent and necessary.

First she showed him the small house with its balcony off the bedroom, where flowers in pots and blossoms hanging from baskets made Johnny feel he was still outdoors. Her father's room had a high tower where he often watched for ships with his telescope.

"What does your father trade in?" he asked, noting a ship's flare on the window sill.

Resa laughed shyly. "The English word is *smuggling*. It is a good business, no?"

Johnny laughed. "If you know how."

"You have money? Good English coin?"

"Yes, of course."

"First we shall have some fun. Do you want to slide the hill?"

Johnny didn't understand. "Slide the hill?"

"One hill is two miles long, and the men pull you up on a toboggan, and you come down fast on the slippery cobblestones. Very much fun. All the sailors like it. You have money?"

"Enough."

The town of Funchal was clean, with a paved street, a cathedral, and a marketplace. Winemaking was a big business, and Johnny watched men load wooden kegs of wine on to a sleigh pulled by bulls. The animals wore a carved piece of bone on their foreheads to ward off the evil eye.

When the wine was loaded, the bulls strained and grunted and pulled the wooden sleigh over the smooth pavement. The men ran in front, throwing down water-soaked rags to help the sleigh move and prevent it from catching fire from friction.

"Hola! Hola!" they cried, waving to the sailors. All the people were friendly and cheerful. Johnny wished he could stay forever.

Down the street trotted three men looking like overgrown porcupines. They carried wine in animal skins slung over their backs. The feet of the animals were still attached to the skins. Johnny thought it the funniest sight he had seen in a long time.

Johnny and Resa walked arm in arm through the sunshine. "Stay here, Juan," Resa coaxed. "You can work with my father. He will like you. I will hide you until the ship sails."

Johnny gazed at all the beauty around him—waving palms, feathery tops of banana trees, the odor of tulips, the green of willows—and thought he might be dreaming. Who would want to go back to a ship, always cold and wet, always hungry, overworked.

Johnny paid in good English cash, and they rode on horseback up a steep road. A little horse boy called a *urriqueiro* held on to each horse's tail to guide it and every so often poked the horses' back legs with a sharp stick.

"Like riding through a vineyard," Johnny said to Resa. Grape vines grew from one side of the road, up poles, overhead, then down the other side of the road. Huge, velvety bunches of grapes, one and two feet long, hung within reach. The vines sagged with their load. Insects with golden wings lit on Resa's arms and head and fluttered around Johnny's face.

"Paradise, paradise," he said over and over. Higher and higher the horses climbed. Johnny, looking down, saw deep gorges and lush green valleys. Chestnut trees with heavy branches shaded them. Lilies bloomed everywhere. Lilacs and roses, ruby-red leaves and camel-brown moss.

Resa stopped the horses to show him the prickly-pear cactus that grew along the edge of the cliff. "Do you see him?" she demanded.

Johnny followed her pointing finger and saw a spider as big as his hand, striped like a zebra, on the cactus. The spider stepped from one thorn to the next, dragging a thick rope it had spun.

"Isn't he a funny fellow? He makes a big, big web to catch the poor bugs and butterflies."

Resa brought her horse close to his. "Is it not beautiful here? The soil is dark loam fed by wells. No rain ever falls. Sometimes a cloud bumps against the mountaintop, breaks apart, and the water pours down into the dry riverbed. Water for the gardens also comes down from the hills, in trenches. We eat, work a little, play much, love. . . ."

Johnny still couldn't believe there was such a spot on earth. After England, with its drizzling chills, wetness, freezing winters, after ship life, it was paradise.

Down in the harbor Johnny saw enormous porpoises jumping and playing. Flocks of pigeons wheeled in curves and scattered all over the rocks. "They are so tame," said Resa, "you can reach out your hand and catch one for cooking."

After their ride, Resa showed him the marketplace, in a grove of trees. Women in long skirts, frilly, laced vests, white kerchiefs covering their heads, brought things to sell—oranges, lemons, figs, pomegranates, pears, melons, pumpkins. Fresh fish, in all colors of the rainbow, were layered on tables. A man in knee breeches and boots played the *machettinho,* an instrument like a guitar. Some of the women formed circles and began to dance.

After that they fished for eels on the rocks. Johnny plunged into the deliciously warm water in a cove and dove until he caught six eels. With no other place to keep them, he put the eels in his sailor's hat, then jammed it down on his head and tied it with his neckerchief, coming down under his chin. Resa laughed until she cried and fell down in the soft sand between two sheltering rocks. Johnny lay beside her, and they talked for a while; then he threw away the eels and put his arm around her. She was soft and willing and her black eyes grew bigger until they were all he could see. The tangerine flush of her cheeks spread as he kissed her.

Afterward, she lay on her side with her eyes closed. Johnny sat hunched over, running the sand through his hand and thinking. He didn't love the girl by his side, but he loved the island paradise, and he hated the ship. What more could a man ask?

They swam together as the fading sun slipped behind the mountain and dusk closed in on the village. The sky changed from peach to pearl. All the men were back on board. He wouldn't be missed for a while, Steenie would see to that.

"You will stay, Juan." Resa laid her head on his shoulder as they lingered on the beach.

Johnny marveled that the night was not chilly or damp, but just as beautiful as the daytime. His old friends, the stars, lit up one by one.

"Let me show you something that happens only when it is winter in England," Resa said. "I will show you a rainbow at night. Ah, you have not seen such a thing, no? Watch now, and you will see what we call the midnight rainbow."

Johnny gazed up. He saw Venus shining with a heavenly glow. He saw the full moon sitting gently on the horizon. Suddenly he saw it as he turned his head slightly. A perfect rainbow arching up over the moon, all the colors plainly seen.

Resa stroked his face. "Is it not lovely? Did we not have a lovely time together today? Will you come with me now? We will sleep in the tower room at home."

"Your father's room?" Johnny was startled. "Let's just sleep under the stars or walk a while."

"No!" Her voice turned steely, then she was all smiles and clinging arms again. "The tower room is so cool, my Juan. Before we sleep we will have a nice glass of sweet wine."

A warning clicked in Johnny's brain. He remembered the flare on the windowsill of the tower room. "I see just the spot for sleep," he said. "Over there, under that tree. You can fetch a blanket from the house to lie on."

She drew away from him coldly. "I do not sleep out on the sand. We will sleep in the tower room."

How many sailors had she drugged with wine? How many deserting seamen had she collected reward money on? How many men had lain in her arms?

He'd swim to the ship, and faithful Steenie would be watching for him. Without a word he plunged into the surf, and just before he ducked under he looked up. The North Star glittered like a diamond afire.

Polly! Oh, Polly!

7

To the Windward Coast

She was scudding along at six knots, with a stiffish breeze, picking up the trade winds. Clear sky. Puffy white clouds every so often. The H.M.S. *Harwich* had been ordered to separate from the fleet and look for enemy ships farther south.

Johnny, up in the crow's nest, looked alert, scanning the horizon. Below, the coopers worked, making water casks. The carpenters sawed squares of wood slabs, ready for patching up holes made from enemy fire. The blacksmith welded a broken iron spar. The man at the wheel kept a sharp eye on the compass. The wind was changing.

She'll run under half sail before the day's over, Johnny predicted to himself. *There's a storm brewing ahead.* A whirly wind circled in under the waves, spinning the spume like egg whites.

He signaled with his arms to the other man aloft, who signaled down to the bosun. Johnny steadied his telescope on the edge of the platform railing and scanned around in a circle. Ho! Off the port side! A ship! Whose?

"Ship, ho!" he sang out. "Over to port! Can't see her colors!"

The bosun summoned the mate, who climbed aloft to look.

83

"Run down our ensign," he ordered, "until we see who she is."

The flag came down, the men took battle stations and shoved the big guns through open portholes. Johnny cursed the luck that put him aloft just when the wind was blowing harder and a strange ship in the offing.

Captain Drummond paced the main deck, his hair neatly done in curls hanging behind his ears. Ned and Ralph and Chester lined up with the other midshipmen.

Johnny examined the oncoming ship. She was big, at least two hundred feet in length, with a gunwale around the hull, so she was a man-of-war. *She's flying our flag,* Johnny noted to himself, *but by my bones she's no friend.*

The wind drove the ships closer together until they were sailing parallel. She was flying a red cross of Saint George and the Ensign Red, and a Canton White at the upper corner next to the staff. *Strange,* Johnny mused, *she's flying merchantman flags. Is she French in disguise? Spanish?*

Now the sky was burdened with dark clouds, and the riggers swarmed up the ratlines to furl sail. But if they furled sail to wait out the storm, how could they escape from an enemy ship? Johnny cursed again and desperately wished himself anywhere but where he was.

Both ships were sailing hard on the wind. The riggers worked like madmen. Apparently the captain had given orders to get away from the other ship, but the ship bore down on them. At the same time a belch and crash of fire from the strange ship hit them, and shot flew through the rigging.

She ran up her true colors, and she was a buccaneer ship! *Pirates.*

Surrender! her flags signaled.

Captain Drummond answered with a mighty broadside blast from all the cannon. Pirates attacking a man-of-war! Johnny started down the ratlines, along with the riggers, and the mast swayed and dipped with the ship's roll. Cold rain hammered his face and arms and weighed down his canvas jacket.

Cannon boomed on both ships, and he knew the *Harwich*

was fighting to put distance between them. The mast shook with each volley, and Johnny tore out all the nails of his right hand trying to keep from falling.

Above the demon screams of the wind Johnny heard grapeshot hitting the mast, ripping sails, breaking yards. The storm broke with the noise of forty wars. The black sea heaved. The other ship slid into a gouged-out hollow in the sea and vanished.

Johnny's feet touched the deck, and he ran to help Ned, who was down on one knee, struggling in the icy brine. "My shoulder hit," he groaned as Johnny helped him up and grabbed a lifeline to support them.

Just then a ton of foaming water washed in from the port side and swept them toward the gunwale, up and over. Johnny still held the lifeline, but Ned was wrenched out of his grasp and hurled overboard.

"Man overboard!" Johnny screamed, sliding through the slimy muck on deck. "Help! Help!" He slid into Ralph, held on to him, and shouted, "Launch the jolly boat! Man overboard! Ned! Hurry! Give the order!"

Ralph fought loose from him. "No! Get below, you fool!"

Johnny, sobbing and cursing, felt as though his lungs would burst from the driving wind. He hardly knew how he got below, half drowned, bleeding from a gash in his leg, weeping for Ned. Steenie found him lying on his face, in the water under his hammock, and lifted his head.

"Up, Johnny! Chester, help me! His leg's torn open, the bone sticking straight out! Carry him off to the surgeon!" Steenie took his arms, and Chester took his ankles. Johnny found himself carted aft to the midshipmen's mess table. The table, covered with a dirty sheet, served as operating table. At sight of the saw in the surgeon's hand, Johnny yelled and fought. Six men had to hold him down.

"Aye, a brave blade," said the surgeon. "Got some lead into him? Or just a scratch?"

"Fell," Johnny blubbered. "My leg's not broken, I tell you! Please don't cut it off!"

The surgeon laughed. "I can see no bone, lad. Just split open. I'll be sewing you up, if Mr. Corner will oblige."

The purser uncorked a bottle of rum and gave Johnny two long swigs. The surgeon began to sew with needle and thread as the men held Johnny down. The purser gave him more rum, then let him bite on the bottle neck so he wouldn't scream.

"As good as new," the doctor beamed, leaning over him. "Has he pulses? Aye, loud as a clock. Next!"

Johnny was carried back to his hammock, where he lay for three days. *Why Ned?* his brain cried over and over. *Why Ned? How did I ever escape?*

On the fourth morning Ralph came looking for him. "Get up, Young John," he said roughly. "Mate says you go back to work."

"Leg hurts," Johnny mumbled, half asleep.

"Get up!" Ralph shook the hammock. "It pleasures me to see you hurt!"

Johnny kept his eyes and mouth closed and hoped Ralph would go away.

"Up, I say!" Ralph drew his knife and sawed at the rope. The hammock broke, and Johnny hit the floor. A stab of pain sliced his sore leg, but he dared not answer.

Up on deck a ship drifted off the port side, and two men from her jolly boat climbed on board.

"What's happening?" Johnny asked a man.

"She's a slaver heading for Sierra Leone. Had trouble with those two men and putting them on board here for punishment. Their captain says he'll take two of ours in return."

Johnny's heart leaped in his chest. He ran to the lieutenant supervising the transfer and fell on his knees. "Mr. Raub, sir! Let me go in their place! Please, oh, please, send me off to the other ship!"

The lieutenant gave him a look of pity. "All right, lad. Maybe you can do better on the slaver. Go along. Take that old one with you."

Steenie! Johnny, faint with joy and pain in his leg, clambered over the side and down into the jolly boat, grinning at Steenie. What luck! Was it possible? The coast of Africa! He'd be back to England within two years!

Steenie ran below for their sea chests and came back with one over each shoulder. "I have everything," he said. Then to the oarsmen, "Hurry! Hurry! Before the old croak changes 'is mind!"

Even as Johnny crossed the swells to the *Bertha*, a slave ship, he was thinking, *No one will know me on this ship. I can do as I please.*

Captain Nunnamin welcomed them briefly. He was a thin, sad-looking man, his eyes like shuttered windows, as though he looked inward. "Both able seamen?" he asked. "Good. We can use you aloft." His first mate took the captain's arm and led him away. "Something out of joint there," Steenie said in a low tone to Johnny. "He's about as steady as a sheet in the wind. Methinks the captain is a sick man."

They were in time for breakfast and lined up with the other men. "How's she vittled?" Steenie asked the man next to him. The fellow held his nose. "Pease pudding," he said. "Pease pudding in the morning, pease pudding at noon, pease pudding at night. Oncet we had an egg. A year ago, if my memory serves me. Aye, pease pudding. Sundays, too," he added, as an afterthought.

The galley was extra large, with an iron stove that could roast a whole pig and turn out eighty pounds of ship biscuit a day. Fueled by coal and charcoal, the stove had a four-inch-high railing to keep the kettles from sliding off. In a copper pot boiled a gallon of water for the ship's surgeon. There was a gross, doggy smell as men in wet clothes pushed together to keep warm.

Each of the thirty-man crew carried his own tin dish and spoon and mug that he had purchased in some old tinker's shop back home. The men passed single file through the galley, then took their meal back to their quarters or, in fine weather, to the deck.

There were still eight men ahead of Johnny when he heard a voice from the dead! Singsonging, complaining, crooning, chuckling, outraged, rascally Old Burgoo! Johnny trod smartly on his neighbor's heels to look ahead.

"By thunder! I'll be sluiced!" Johnny swore happily. "The dickens himself fetch me to a hot bed if it ain't Old Burgoo! Steenie, it's Old Burgoo!"

"I'll split yer nose," threatened the man in front of Johnny, "if you don't leave off a-standin' on my heels!"

"Pease porridge, my lovelies. Oh, Old Burgoo wouldn't lie to ye, no, not by his liver and gizzard. Today it's baked to a turn, lads, lightly browned on the edges, aye, baked in a scallop shell and dabbed with cream! Old Burgoo was up all night a-bakin' of the pease porridge, me hearties. Do have a bit of porridge afore the roast leg-o'-mutton, dearies."

Johnny and Steenie clapped the cook on the back and pumped his arm up and down. They stared into one anothers' eyes. "You're not ghosts?" Burgoo inquired. "Faith, lads, I never thought to see you again. Oh, I was washed off the deck all right and tossed right up on the next ship, washed off again, picked up by a jolly boat, taken to shore, and joined the slaver."

Burgoo stopped, out of breath. "Best move along now. I'll hunt ye when I'm off duty."

Johnny drank the lukewarm pea soup and ate his flour biscuit. "What's she carrying?" he asked a sailor.

"Rum and gin," was the answer. "She'll pick up slaves in Africa."

"How's the captain?"

The sailor gave him a queer look. "Ye seen how he was. His days is numbered short. He lies a-bed with the opium pipe, and the mate gives the orders. We'll be in a pretty pickle when we get that load of ebony aboard. I was in a mutiny oncet, but don't hope to be in it twicet."

As Johnny put his sea chest in order he found the book *Rhapsody* and threw it overboard. In doing that, he threw away the last thing he believed in. If there was no right or wrong, no heaven or hell, as Ned said, then he would do as he pleased. If death ended all, why not?

He thought of the narrow escapes from death he'd had, many of them. He remembered the dream. There almost seemed to be a hand directing his life. Almost. Now he could laugh at the idea.

He didn't waste any time inquiring for men interested in smuggling, gambling, and all manner of evil. He attracted them as the north pole pulls the magnet.

Steenie saw what was happening. "Johnny," he said one day as they sat carving to pass the time, "you've clean sold yourself to the evil one."

Johnny spit out a choice oath.

"You've a heart of flint. I do believe you took leave of your conscience."

"And you're a bellyful of wind," Johnny said crudely. "Do you want to know how much money I've made selling the cargo to the crew while you sat around hymn singing and Bible reading?"

"You didn't tap the casks?"

"Right you are. Sucked out the rum with a hollow quill, spit it into bottles Burgoo got me, sold 'em for tuppence each. What a rare joke when the old opium eater finds twenty casks half empty."

Fair weather followed them most of the way. One afternoon late in the dogwatch, the men were idling on deck around the capstan, bored, and Johnny was spoiling for some fun. The officers were below, sleeping no doubt, and the captain in a stupor. Fine ship!

Johnny sprang up on the capstan and began to sing, making up verses as he went. A fiddler took up a screechy tune, and two sailors with flutes attempted to follow along.

> "Oh, a captain sailed the waters as calm as could be
> And his voyage brought him along the China Sea;
> And when his business with pigtails was all done
> He brought back a mistress named op-i-um!"

"And he brought back a mistress named op-i-um!" roared the sailors.

Johnny started them clapping and tapping their feet.

> "Now the ship sails in circles, a lubber's in command,
> We're all doomed fellows, but a jolly band;
> The crew lives on knuckles and pickled tripe
> And the captain takes to bed with his dreamy pipe."

"And the captain takes to bed with his dreamy pipe!" sang the men.

"The poor captain's dying . . . ," Johnny added some words that shocked even the worst of them, but he couldn't stop. He felt a madness overpower him, and his mouth was out of control. He began to jig and whirl in a tight circle, and Old Burgoo and some of the others joined him. Louder and louder he bawled the dirty words.

Suddenly he was the only one singing. He nearly tripped over his feet as he braked and looked up. The captain and mate had been standing by the taffrail, along the stern deck, and heard it all.

Captain Nunnamin's face was gray and pulled down to twice its length, like warm taffy. "Mr. Newton." He spoke slowly and groped for words. "Mr. Newton, sir, you will be—be—put aboard. . . ."

". . . put aboard the first man-of-war we meet," the mate finished briskly, giving Johnny a hateful look. "Captain's orders. No more skylarking aboard this ship. You men there go on half rations for a week."

Johnny took his turn on watch that night and paced the deck, composing a letter to Polly in his mind.

Polly, dearest darling girl, I have thought of nothing else since I met you. My love for you will never end. It is stronger than death, more beautiful than any poem ever written. Polly, I adore you. Your eyes. . . . He stopped to consider. *Her eyes. Green like the sea? Blue like the sky?* He couldn't remember, except that when he looked at her he melted inside.

He paced fore and aft, from port to starboard. He looked at the North Star. Was she looking? No, she went abed by nine, and it was after midnight.

Polly, love, most precious Polly, I will come back a rich man, and you will have everything you want. We will own a house and drive a fine carriage and take tea together afternoons at four, and I will love you. . . .

He leaned for a while on the ship's railing, biting his broken, dirty fingernails. *Polly, Polly.* He could almost see her right now beside him, her little face lifted up to his, her hair a waterfall down her back, gleaming like polished brass.

Such a longing swept over him that he felt ill. Better not to think. He paced and the hours passed and he went below and by the light of a candlestub wrote: "Dear Polly, I am on the slave ship *Bertha,* heading for West Africa. The weather is fine. We are doing well. I trust your mother and Catherine and all are well. Please write if you are able. I think of you. I am sincerely and obediently yours, John Newton."

Four months passed, the days all alike. Johnny kept ears and eyes open for a man-of-war, for he determined to throw himself into the sea and drown rather than be transferred.

As they sailed along the west coast of Africa the air changed into warm breezes and stifled them. The men grew lazy and longed for more than their ration of a quart of water a day. Most of them slept on the deck at night to catch a breeze. By day, the sun dried them out like tinder. The salted meat crazed their thirst, and they licked sweat from one anothers' faces. Afternoons the heat throbbed in their heads like jungle drums.

The first mate turned nasty and flogged men for the slightest fault. One day he flipped a silver piece into the air and said, "For the man who sights land!"

That aroused some interest, and one morning a sailor named Gilbert shouted, "Land, ho!" and backed down the ratlines to claim his prize. Mr. Radshaw, the first mate, flipped the coin to tease him and said, "No, sir, I spied land one hour ago. Two dozen lashes for you, sir, to reward your laziness."

Gilbert was tied in the shroud ropes and whipped. Mr. Radshaw dashed a bucket of salt-and-peppered water on his wounds, and Gilbert lay in the brutal sun, crying for a drink.

The men hated the mate, and Johnny wondered what would happen when Mr. Radshaw discovered the half-empty casks. He'd marked each one with a spot of chalk, and maybe if he helped roll them ashore, they wouldn't be noticed until the ship sailed.

The ship continued down the coast past Cape Verde and anchored at Sierra Leone. Johnny was getting his first look at the slave trade. A slave station, a thrown-together old warehouse, rotted alongside the Sherbro River, which crawled with alligators. A human chain of slaves shuffled down a jungle trail from the mountains, guarded by black traders toting guns and spears. African chiefs, Johnny heard from an old sailor, rid themselves of enemies and prisoners of war by selling them as slaves. Sometimes starving families sold their children. Black criminals were sold into slavery. Families kidnapped by the traders ended up at the slave station. The white trader was only the middleman, arranging the deals.

Terror was carved into the faces of the slaves, as though they believed the ugly white men with sunburned skin were planning to eat them alive. The slaves were chained together by the neck and marched into the wooden barricades to await evening, when the captains would go ashore, bargain, and get happily drunk.

A healthy black man cost 110 gallons of gin, a woman 90. Those of the Ibo people were considered too mournful to be hard workers. The Ashanti were rebellious. The English traders preferred Gold Coast slaves, who worked hard and kept cheerful.

Chiefs, greedy for guns and gin, often attacked their own villages at night and tied up the people for the slave traders. Tribe fought tribe, black nation fought black nation. As they took prisoners they sent them to the slave stations along the coast, where white traders of many nations waited.

Johnny was put to unloading the liquor. Along with Steenie he lashed the kegs securely in the ship's longboat, lowered it over the side, beached it safely on shore. The work took weeks, and Johnny grew weak from the never-ending heat and spoiled food.

Three hundred slaves were shackled down in the cargo hold of the ship, and she was ready to sail. Johnny was standing on the deck with Steenie when he heard it. First, the solemn roll of a drum, on and on, without letup. Then the British ensign lowered to half-mast, then the cannon began firing at thirty-second intervals.

"The captain!" Johnny said in a low tone.

A sailor friend hurried over to them. "Captain Nunnamin's dead," he said. "The mate's in charge and fixin' to put you aboard a man-o'-war, Johnny. Take care."

"My thanks," said Johnny. He grasped Steenie's arm. "I'll die first!" He ripped the string from his neck and gave his friend the key to his sea chest. "You'll find a letter to a Miss Polly Catlett. Put it with the other mail and good luck to you, Steenie. I'll take my chances with the sharks and the cannibals afore I go back on a man-o'-war. I'm going into the slave trade, and I'll come back to England a rich man!"

8

Voodoo Island

Johnny waited until nightfall then slung a rope ladder over the side of the ship and let himself down, striking out into the calm sea. The water was cold and the night cool. In a month the rainy season would begin. He swam easily, and a white-crested breaker swept him to land, rolling him across the sand and brush burning his arms. He might have been shipwrecked, for all he owned were his pants and striped shirt.

The slave station seemed deserted, and he crept inside and curled up in one corner on the ground. Mosquitoes tormented him all night, and the heat made his head throb. At dawn he watched the ship until it was a white blob far out to sea. Now it was safe to look for a white trader and offer to work for him.

He could smell the jungle—misty, moist, steamy. He walked through the compound and found two white men still sleeping. Traders. Kneeling down, he shook them gently. They leaped to their feet, guns in hand.

"I deserted the ship," Johnny said bluntly, knowing he couldn't be returned now. "I'm looking for honest work with a trader. Name's John Newton."

"You gave us a start, you did," said the shorter of the two white men. "Daniel Grubber here, and this is Steve Milto. Well, Johnny, we're following the river inland. Wouldn't recommend it for you. Best if you got to one of the Benanoes Islands. Burt Langerman is looking for help. He's one of the biggest slave dealers around, married to a black princess, he is. You'd do all right working for him."

"How far away is he?"

"Benanoes is twelve leagues to the southeast. Make yourself a raft, take a plank for paddle, and you'll be there before the day is old. Tell him Dan Grubber sent you."

"My thanks." Johnny looked around. "Can you lend me tools or help me?"

The traders began to pack their canvas bags. "We have a long day's trek to meet a chief. We can't stop for man nor devil. The rains will start soon, and the river will flood. You're welcome to break up some of the empty kegs yonder, and you'll find pieces of rope and canvas around." The men nodded in farewell and set out upriver in their native canoe.

"Build a raft!" Johnny said in disgust, after they were out of hearing. "Aye, and a house and veranda, too, while I'm at it!"

He found a keg four feet high and turned it on its side. Using a stone from the beach, he knocked the upper part in and broke the pieces away until he formed a sort of wooden tub to sit in. Broad, leafy ferns grew all around the river, and he piled them into the tub, to use as shelter against the sun. A large, cupped seashell would do for bailing water.

All the time his ears strained for the sound of native war drums and blood-curdling yells. Hurry—hurry—before they saw him!

For a sail he used a square of gray canvas. A rope fastened it between two poles. A barrel stave made a paddle, and he wound extra rope around his waist. Wading into the surf, he dragged his wooden tub. When a breaker rose, he let himself and the tub be lifted, the wave passed under him, and he was launched.

Once far enough out beyond breakers, he eyed the sun and paddled southeast. When he felt a breeze, he raised the clumsy sail, bracing the little mast in the bottom of the tub with his bare feet. He held the top of the sail with both hands. The sail was barely three feet high, but the breeze filled it out, and he sailed along.

When he judged an hour had passed, he eased his aching arms and let the tub drift. For the next hour he again raised the sail and continued this way until noon, resting every hour.

"There she is!" he exclaimed, sighting land. Hungry, horribly thirsty, sun-blistered and hot, he saw the islands. Three of them. He strained toward the largest one.

A powerful wave caught him, flung him high on its crest for a minute, then dashed him down on the beach, smashing the tub and rolling Johnny head over heels on the sand. Gasping to breathe, he crawled out of reach of the waves, then flopped facedown to rest. He heard stealthy feet in the sand but was too exhausted to look up.

A man knelt and rolled him over. "Where'd you come from?"

Johnny looked up and saw a white man in red shirt and black pants, face tough and leathery from the sun, a thin, angry face, thin lips, a few teeth missing, a rough reddish-brown beard down to his chest.

"Deserted ship. Name's Johnny Newton. Looking for work. For Burt Langerman." Johnny sat up slowly and picked sand from his burned arms.

"I'm Burt. How'd you know where to find me?"

"Landed on Sierra Leone. Dan Grubber told me. I could use some vittles and a stiff drink."

The man stared at him in admiration. "You're a bold one, you are. Come along, there's plenty to eat and drink and palm oil for your burns."

Burt took him to a lean-to made of branches and thatch. "I don't live here," he said. "Just stopped by on—uh—business. Another hour and you wouldn't have caught me. I live on the

Plantanes. They're three islands seven leagues further down along the coast. My missus and I live on the largest; it's just two miles across. I can use some help. You ever done slaving?"

"No, but I'll do anything," Johnny said, gulping down the lukewarm water and eating spoiled fruit. "What's the name of your island?"

The man stared at him with his small, glittering brown eyes. "Voodoo Island. Don't let it scare you none; it's just a name."

Johnny shrugged. "I don't scare."

"Not many ships stop in the rainy season that's coming on," said Burt. "Not many slaves now unless there's one of them wars going on. I do expect one ship in a few days, and you can help brand and load."

"Brand?"

"We brand them with the ship's initial letter while they're still on shore; then we board ship and help pack, since I know how better 'n them swabs."

"Pack?"

"Right you are, pack them in the hold. I know ways to pack 'em tight and put four hundred where three hundred used to fit. You'll see."

"What's to do during the rainy season?"

"Not too much. Smuggling, drinking, lying around waiting for the cursed rain to stop. Going to *their* meetings if you like it."

"Their meetings?"

"The blacks who work for me on my plantation of lime trees. They have their voodoo certain nights, and if you like it, you can watch. Last time I watched, I drank for five days and nights, and the missus almost killed me, she was that mad."

Johnny didn't ask anymore. Anything was better than a man-of-war, so he wouldn't quarrel.

"Let's go." Burt jumped up and led the way to his canoe. In a short time they beached at Voodoo Island, which was covered with palm trees. Not far from the sloping, white sand was Burt's house, built out of cement blocks he'd made himself.

with a corrugated iron roof. The lime trees, most only three feet high and not yet bearing fruit, grew in back of the house. The black servants lived in mud huts with grass roofs, a half-dozen families, the women in long, patched dresses and triangular orange squares knotted over their heads, the men in short pants, the children naked as monkeys.

Johnny, damp and sticky with perspiration that would not evaporate, was glad to enter the cool house.

"This is Kiringa," Burt said, indicating a tall, stout black woman dressed in purple cloth, gold earrings, yellow turban. She was spaniel-eyed, tossing her head and squeezing her mouth up in dislike of him. Johnny bobbed his head respectfully but resolved to stay away from her.

"Would you like some brandy? The French liquor is far superior to English gin."

Johnny was surprised at her elegant manners. She was a good cook, too, and he feasted on English dishes he thought he'd never see again.

Burt gave him a small room for himself, and Johnny couldn't believe his good luck. Though it was hot—sirocco hot—the nights were cool for the rains would soon begin. After a few nights of good sleep, he felt better than ever. Burt asked if he wanted to see the voodoo meeting.

The meeting was held in an empty barn on the edge of the plantation. It was smeary dark inside, except for some fat candles stuck in a piece of log at one end of the long room. From the rafters hung decorated wine bottles, driftwood, bunches of feathers, and gourds.

Black men and women sat around the edge of the room, some on benches, most of them hunkered down or cross-legged on the floor.

Johnny noted that one man appeared to be the priest, dressed in an ugly, torn puce robe. He spent the first half hour spilling an intricate pattern over the center of the floor, sifting white meal and ashes through his fingers, dribbling them into the outline of a snake. As the design took shape the women began to chant softly and drums thrummed innocently while the priest made scrolls and symbols and flower knots all around the snake.

The drums picked up a more frantic rhythm, throbbing and pulsating with life, and three orange-skirted women began to dance in a sort of shuffle-hustle, strings of beads rippling over chests. Others joined them, and soon there was a forest of black, writhing arms twisted up together.

The dancers jigged slowly, then rocked to and fro, their feet wiping out the snake pattern.

Johnny strained to see all that went on in the semidarkness and felt as if he were being drawn into the ceremony. The priest sacrificed six roosters, cutting off their heads and catching the blood in a bowl, which was passed around for the dancers to drink.

Faster and faster beat the drums. The dancers moaned and swayed. Something alive entered the barn and took possession of them. Johnny was belted across the face with the warm, feathered body of a chicken, and the blood dripped onto his shirt. One by one the dancers screamed and twirled as evil spirits entered them, and they fell down as dead. Kiringa stood alone, her body a turning spit over an invisible fire. Johnny felt a madness fill his brain, and he knew if he didn't get away from there, he would never be sane again.

He fought his way out of the barn and bumped into Burt waiting for him. "Had enough?"

Johnny thumped his head to clear it and took Burt's arm. "Why—why do they do it?"

As they groped their way through the lime trees rain belted down, lightning snaked at them, and thunderclaps threatened to lay them flat.

Inside the house, Johnny repeated, "Why?"

"Why? Nothing else to do," Burt said, lighting a pipe. "A demon comes into them, and they feel good. That's religion. Keeps them out of mischief during the rainy spell. My black overseer, Bunto, keeps them under control otherwise. We all get along fine here."

That week a black runner visited them to say a string of slaves in chains were waiting at the warehouse at Cape Mount, on the mainland. The American brig, *Sally*, from Rhode Island anchored offshore.

Burt owned a Bullom boat, small with a triangular sail, named after the tribe in Africa, who were skillful seamen. He showed Johnny how to sail it, and early one morning they skimmed across the sea to Cape Mount.

Burt paid cash to the black trader who waited for him. That evening the captain came ashore and looked the slaves over. He paid in kegs of rum for two hundred but refused twenty who were older and had an eye disease.

"What will happen to them?" asked Johnny.

Burt waved him away. "Turn them loose. There won't be another ship along for six months."

One of the black men ran to a woman who was chained, threw his arms around her, and tried to pry the chain off her neck. Four children were chained to her, and Johnny took them for a family.

The slaves for the ship were herded into the compound made of mud and the twenty useless ones shooed away. They disappeared into the brush. All except the man who wanted his family. He howled around the compound for hours until Burt spoke a word to the foreman, who went outside.

Johnny heard the crack of a gun, and the tormented howling ceased. He had seen sailors flogged to death, but this was quick murder. The hair stood up along his neck, and a shuddering chill ran down his arms. Burt was someone to fear.

Early in the morning a fire was built and the ship's brand heated white-hot. One by one the slaves passed by, and Burt touched their right shoulders with a drop of oil, then pressed the hot iron into the skin. Most of the slaves made no sound, such was their terror.

"You try it, now," Burt ordered, putting the branding iron in Johnny's hand. The first time his hand trembled, and the black man jumped back in pain. Johnny didn't relish burning helpless people, especially women and children, but he didn't want Burt to think he wasn't hard. After a while he lost all feeling about it. He worked away as if he were branding animals. Even the children refused to utter a sound.

They were loaded forty to a canoe and taken out to the ship's longboat, which came to meet them. While being transferred, the men suddenly went wild and tried to jump overboard and drown themselves. Four of them almost succeeded, and Burt was obliged to send a man after them, with ropes.

The blacks fought, kicking with their feet, keeping their heads under, but when they tired, they were roped around the waist and pulled into the longboat. Each slave drowned meant 110 gallons of rum wasted.

On board ship the slaves were hosed down with water, their gums scrubbed to prevent disease, and they were allowed a meal of beans and Indian corn porridge, called "dabbadabb."

Burt and the captain put their heads together over the paper plans of the cargo hold. There was space in the hold for only 150 slaves, lying side by side on wooden planks.

"Turn them on their sides like spoons," Burt told the captain. "Pack them together that way, and they'll fit. No need to let them up on deck for exercise. Other captains don't do it. Danger of mutiny that way. Pass the buckets of food along from each end, and they'll feed themselves.

"And if they wish to retire to the water closet . . . ?" the captain was being tactful.

"Don't bother," Burt grunted. "Hose them off twice a week."

"On my last trip through the Middle Passage to the Indies they wouldn't eat," the captain complained. "Lost near a dozen that starved themselves."

"Touch a hot coal to their lips as a warning," Burt said.

Johnny thought to himself that Burt knew many ways of

punishing people. Burt had told him how his wife had been a princess in her own nation, a woman of wealth and power. She made it possible for Burt to go into business. How did she feel, seeing her own people sold into slavery? Johnny puzzled over it as he waited.

Once down in the hold, the slaves finally realized all hope of seeing their own country was gone, and they began to wail and cry and groan. Johnny helped batten down the hatches, and he heard the pitiful cries for days afterward and in his sleep at night.

Burt noticed his silence, and one day he said, "A man can't be soft in the slave trade. If you're going to work with me, you mustn't pull back when I give an order. I need a man I can depend on."

They were dining, and Kiringa served them coffee with real sugar from the ship, baked bread, fish, yams, and cake with fruit sauce. They ate from china plates, using silver knives, forks, and spoons.

"Made twenty thousand gallons of rum this last time," Burt said, "besides some pistols, muskets, candles, and vittles for Kiringa. We live like kings here, but you better learn to be hard, lad."

"What do you do with the rum?"

"Part of it will buy more slaves, when the rainy season is over. The rest I trade for gold, jewels, ivory, whatever I want. It's all hid lad," he looked sideways at Johnny. "All hid and you'll never see it, but I'll go back to England some day. That's what I live for."

Kiringa slapped down a plate of biscuits and a dish of honey. "The day you go back to England," she said scornfully to Burt, "that day I become queen of the continent."

Johnny understood her to mean she would never let Burt get away. Burt talked long into the night, drinking and smoking, eating too much. "England will fight France soon," he said. "That will slow down the slave trade. When that happens, I'll

make money selling guns to the warring tribes. After that. . . .
Some day . . . ," His head dropped down on his folded arms.
He was sound asleep.

Johnny wrote a short note to Polly. "Dear Polly, I am living
on one of the Plantane Islands, off the West Coast of Africa. I
am in business now and making a fair living. The weather is
warmer than in England, and there is plenty to eat. I hope to
be back before two years are gone. Yours, John Newton." Mail
was given to any ship that stopped and was passed from ship to
ship until it reached its destination.

Before Johnny had a chance to show his new master he
could work hard, he fell ill. Mosquitoes seemed attracted to his
white skin, and after hundreds of bites and infection from
scratching, he took a high fever.

That day Burt sailed to Rio Nuno on business and Johnny
was left in the care of Kiringa. Johnny's head ached; he burned
with fever from head to feet, and his stomach was sick. At first
Kiringa cooked meals, but after a few days grew tired of looking after him. She ordered one of the slaves to move him outdoors, lest she catch his sickness. His bed was a mat on a
wooden board, with a small log for pillow.

Many times he begged for water, when the fever was highest
and his lips cracked and peeling, but Kiringa only laughed at
him. When his appetite returned, he was too weak to get up,
and she sent him no food, though she had plenty. Only twice
she told a slave to take him the garbage left on her plate after
she finished a good dinner.

Johnny was glad to get anything and ate it eagerly, thanking
her. Still, Burt did not return. Many times in the night Johnny
crawled to the field and dug up raw yams and ate them, then
became sick and threw them up.

He would have starved if two of the slaves, hands chained
together, had not brought him some bread from their own
small share, after Kiringa was asleep. If caught, they would
have been beaten.

One day Kiringa called him to come and lick her plate after a meal. Johnny hungrily took the plate, stumbled, and dropped the scraps of food. Kiringa laughed until her heavy gold earrings swung in circles.

Finally the horror dawned on him that he was a slave to this former slave. Day and night he lay out in the weather, suffocating in the humid daytime air, being chilled at night. Every day Kiringa paid him a visit, to mock and laugh at him.

One day she stopped by his mat with five slaves. "Get up and walk!" she commanded. She was almost six feet tall, draped from neck to knee in bright green satin. Her turban was gold and her earrings jade. Johnny pulled himself to his knees, and before he could rise, the slaves began to pelt him with limes, hard as rocks, hitting his face and chest. They clapped their hands and laughed, then stoned him with anything they could find. Johnny, half starved and still sick, tripped and fell, hurting his back. A spasm began in his side, and he bit his lips to keep from groaning.

After dark, when Kiringa was in the house, feasting, one of the slaves crept to where Johnny lay, washed his face, and gave him a drink. Taking a chunk of bread from his shirt, he put it into Johnny's hands, then turned and silently crawled back to the slave pen without his supper.

9

Alone in the Jungle

By the time Burt returned from his trip, Johnny was a six-foot skeleton. His hair and beard were matted and dirty. His pants and shirt were faded from the sun and from washing and scraping them clean in the creek with a flat stone.

The slaves pitied him and many times shared their bread with him, when Kiringa wasn't looking.

Twice a ship's longboat stopped and Johnny hid in the field, ashamed to be seen in his filth and misery.

He wrote a letter to his father, asking him again to forgive him and send for him. The third time a ship's longboat stopped, Johnny ran out from the woods and begged one of the sailors to take the letter. His pride kept him from asking the sailors for help. Also he was a deserter and could be tried and hung.

He tried to explain to Burt how he was treated in his absence. Kiringa just stood by, scornfully, and lied to her husband. "Does he look like he has been working hard?" she demanded. "Oh, my, a fine companion you rescued from the

107

sea! An idle piece of driftwood! He has lain in the shade, asking for his favorite dainties, then refused them. He's a vicious, wild animal if you cross him.''

Burt angrily refused to speak to him for a few days, and Johnny continued to sleep outdoors like a slave. The thought of seeing Polly again kept him alive. He passed the long days by drawing geometry figures in the sand with a stick, trying to remember what he had learned long ago.

Kiringa put him to work planting more young lime trees. "Only to think that someday you will go back to England rich as a lord," she mocked him. "You'll get command of a fine ship and come back to visit us. By then these little trees will be big trees, and you can pick limes, the fruit of your labor.'' She laughed at her joke. "How happy we'll be to entertain you. No doubt you have a young lady waiting for you at home.''

Polly. Johnny said nothing and worked on hands and knees until dark. Burt never did mention what his pay would be. *Polly.* Would he ever see her again? Not as a rich man, he knew.

Finally Burt relented and told him they were taking a trip. "Slaves have been scarcer than icicles," he said wryly. "You and I are going to stir up a little trouble, Johnny-boy.''

They stowed their gear aboard his Bullom sailboat, the *Daisy*, along with fifty kegs of the rum and twenty muskets. "We need a tribal war," Burt said. "We'll anchor at the mainland, then take the canoe up the Jong River and trek back into the bush a ways. I know where the Orba tribe worships at their sacred hollow tree. Looky here,'' he said, pulling a weird object from a canvas bag.

All Johnny could make of it was a bunch of colored feathers with three small rattling gourds tied in the middle, a broken twig, and a ribbon.

"What's that?'' he asked, as the ship, *Daisy*, filled sail and moved out to sea.

"A sort of hex-curse thing from the Kenti tribe. Kiringa remembered how to make it. *You* drop it at the Orba sacred tree; *they* think the Kenti did it—and we have our tribal war."

"*I?*" said Johnny alarmed. "Did you say *I* go there?"

Burt looked as cunning as a vixen that just devoured its own young ones. "Yes, I said *you.* I'll point you on the right trail, and when you come back, I'll reward you handsomely. We'll show the guns and rum to both tribes and offer them in return for slaves. A ship or two may yet stop by before the rainy season."

They anchored the *Daisy* at Bonthe, a town behind the Island of Sherbro, where the Jong River emptied into the ocean. A one-hundred-year-old English-built fort jutted out over the harbor, a place where slavers and traders and sea captains met to bargain.

Along the coast they could see bushy mangrove swamps and plains of green hills, behind that, the jungle and mountains of mahogany and cottonwood trees.

One of Burt's contacts, Clyde Wickett, was waiting for them. His round face was set atop a fat, red neck. His sly, blue eyes were protected by glasses, and there was a droop to one side of his mouth. Johnny decided he didn't like him any more than he liked Burt.

"Stay aboard and keep a weather eye open," Burt said to Clyde. "I'll introduce Johnny here to the jungle." He carried the canvas bag with the hex feathers, jugs of water, and some bread. He took a gun for himself, but refused one to Johnny.

The Jong River looped its way through dense swamp and back into soggy, steamy, tangled, strangling jungle. Johnny knelt on one knee in the bottom of the canoe and helped paddle. It was like rowing through molasses. They were struggling upriver, and the flow of the water pulled them back. Currents, mounds of weeds and slime, underwater creatures, all tried to prevent any movement. "It's not very far," Burt volunteered after a half hour. "Once we land, the forest opens up, and you won't have trouble walking. The sacred tree is about a mile.

Elephants and monkeys around, but they won't bother you."

A feeling of terror came over Johnny, and he could hardly draw breath enough to paddle. "You—you've been there?" he stuttered. "Why can't you come with me?"

"Only takes one," Burt drawled. "Don't fret, I'll be waiting. Wouldn't lose a good, hard-working slave."

Slave! There it was again. He was trapped. Burt knew he'd deserted ship and could never hope for escape.

Burt guided the canoe on to a mudbank, eased himself out, and together they pulled it higher onto the land. "Big alligator almost got me here last time," Burt said. He handed Johnny the canvas bag and told him to take a good drink of water and eat something.

"I should have the gun," Johnny said desperately.

"You're safer without a weapon," Burt replied calmly. "The natives know me, and they know white men. You'll be all right, but don't potter along, be quick about it. I don't fancy the sun setting on me in the jungle."

"Why couldn't I mind the boat and you go, since you know the way?" Johnny hated to move from the safety of the mudbank.

Burt grew angry. "You blasted sea monkey! Follow that trail for one mile, keep the sun on your left. You will come to a circle of big cottonwoods with a hollow one in the center. Drop the hex feathers right down in front and hurry back." He leveled the gun at Johnny. "I'll tell you when you get back why I won't go there anymore."

Johnny backed away from Burt until there was a bend in the trail; then he turned and jogged along, thinking any minute a bullet would cut him down. Everything was quiet, except for shrill bird cries. Orchids, white, pink, lavender, hung in garlands around the tree trunks. Surprisingly, the jungle air was cool and the moss underfoot soft to his bare feet.

The trail was easy to follow. He judged he must have covered a half mile when he suddenly felt as though he were being watched. He looked behind him. Nothing. No one. He stopped dead and looked to the right and left, his eyes wandering up and down the trees and tangled vines overhead. Nothing and no one.

He was alone, but he felt crowded, the same feeling he had at the voodoo meeting on Burt's plantation. *Don't panic,* he thought. *Aye, imagination can cast spells, too!*

He walked slowly, but the closer he came to the grove of cottonwood trees, the more smothered he felt. Finally he could not bear the feeling of descending into a pit of evil, and he stopped. No closer. Burt would never know.

Without remembering to open the canvas bag, he threw it as hard as he could straight forward, then turned and ran back down the trail. He ran until his chest blew up with pain, and at last he raced out of the jungle and down to the mud bar where Burt sat, smoking and fanning himself with his hat.

"You're back sooner than I thought." Burt looked at him suspiciously and handed him a paddle.

"D-didn't want to keep you—keep us—here after dark."

Burt grinned and showed his broken teeth and the empty space where his pipe fit. They shoved off from shore. "You felt the evil, didn't you? Now you know why I won't go there again. Raved like I was out of my head for a week afterward. Kiringa had to give me a few drops of opium and some of her other native mixtures."

An alligator bumped them, then dove, scraping his rough hide on the underside of the canoe. They rocked violently and almost capsized.

"Hold on, there! Where is it?" Burt paused with lifted paddle and stared at Johnny. "Where's the canvas bag?"

"The b-bag—oh, I dropped it when I ran. Didn't think you wanted it."

Burt swung his paddle close to Johnny's head. "You young devil! I knew you came back too soon. You never went near the grove, did you? You just threw the hex in the bushes, did you? Curse you for a snively, cowardly girl! I'll tend to you when we get back. Aye, I'll reward you, I will!"

The canoe followed the current downriver, and in a short while they were back at Bonthe and the *Daisy*. Burt forced him aboard at gunpoint and called Clyde, who was sleeping below.

"We'll wait a long while for slaves now, thanks to Johnny-boy," Burt said angrily as he told what happened. The two of them shackled Johnny by one leg to an iron ring on the deck, then went below to drink. Johnny lay for hours under the afternoon sun, trying to shield his head with his cupped hands.

Burt came back up on deck, staggering and smelling of rum. "We'll anchor here a month or two," he said. "I'll be selling you to the first trader that promises to give you to one of them cannibals. Aye, I'll reward you for all the trouble you made. A cann-i-bal chief . . . a hungry—." He keeled over, dead drunk.

Clyde dragged him below, snarling to himself. Darkness fell, and Johnny felt the kiss of rain on his face. The rains were beginning. The wind blew almost hurricane force, and the little boat rocked and twisted. Johnny was rolled back and forth on the deck as far as his chain would permit.

All night he lay in the cold water that collected on deck, dressed only in his worn pants and shirt. Hour after hour rain beat down upon him. He shivered so that sleep was impossible. He felt as if he were sprawled at the bottom of the world, the lowest of creatures, a worm, with all the trouble and pain of the universe washing over him.

In the morning Burt gave him a pint of rice for the day and some chicken entrails for bait to fish. Johnny could walk six feet in each direction, with his right leg in irons. The chain was long enough to allow him to fish over the side of the boat, and at slack water, when the tide was changing, he threw a line over and sometimes caught a fish.

He thought there was nothing so delicious as the raw fish eaten without bread or drink. Sometimes he didn't catch a fish, and there was nothing to do but curl up in a ball and try to sleep. Burt left him alone in the rain and wind for as long as forty hours at a time.

Day and night the wind blew a gale, and the rain never

stopped, but fell in torrents. Johnny's fever returned, and he was never without pain in his arms and legs. For eight weeks Burt left him chained on deck, like a dumb brute, in all kinds of bad weather.

Johnny's only thought of God was: *If the Christian religion is true, then it's not for me, for I am the worst sinner that ever lived.* Over and over his thoughts tormented him: *I am so bad that not even God Himself could help me. He would never listen to a prayer from me. There is no hope for me.*

Once he prayed to Polly, trying to picture her, thousands of miles away in Kent, sitting cozily by the fireplace, reading his short letter. When his mind was raving mad from fever, he called her name over and over. When the deeps of the ocean were astir like a sea monster, lashing the ship with icy waves, he called her name.

After two months Burt released him to help cut down trees around his house on Voodoo Island. Johnny worked hard, hating his master and planning how to get away.

He heard of a new slave trader, Dick Pocket, who lived on the other side of the island. He asked Burt over and over for permission to go and work for Mr. Pocket, and over and over Burt said no.

One morning he overheard Kiringa talking to Burt. "Send him away," she commanded. "You've had enough work out of him. He's sickly and lazy, and I can't abide the sight of him. If you don't get rid of him now, he'll get uppity and demand payment for his work."

"Go," Burt said to him afterward. "You're of no use to me anymore."

Johnny dropped his shovel and without a word hiked two miles over to the other side of the island. He had been a slave for fifteen months.

Dick Pocket was a wealthy slave trader who owned several slave "factories" on other islands and along the Kittam River. Tall, white-haired, he was as friendly and kind as Burt had been mean and cruel. The first thing he did was send Johnny for a bath and assigned two black slaves to dress him in new clothes. His cook prepared a feast, and at the table Mr. Pocket talked about himself. He had commanded a ship years ago.

"Rheumatiz pains in my joints are a bother," he said, piling his plate with broiled fish and rice. "I can use a young lad like you to be overseer and do book work and travel for me. Have you studied math?"

Johnny delighted Pocket with his knowledge of algebra and geometry. Johnny felt so much better after a hair trim and in gentleman's clothes.

"You're well rid of Burt Langerman," Mr. Pocket went on. "Aye, a pretty life that must have been for a merchant commander's son."

"I'll serve you well, sir," Johnny promised him. His hopes soared. He would yet return to England a rich man.

Soon he was trusted with all the bookkeeping. He handled thousands of English bank notes and paid bills and wrote out orders. Mr. Pocket trusted him completely and paid him well. Johnny saved all his money. He lived in comfort and was often invited to dine with other slave traders.

Mr. Pocket's housekeeper was a partly white girl he had named Claire. Though she worked in the garden and cooked, she also read books and made jewelry and did beadwork. They often sat and talked evenings, when the work was done, and Mr. Pocket encouraged the friendship.

Claire had an English pointy little nose and straight brown hair, but her skin was a lovely tan, her eyes large and brown, fringed with curly lashes. She was shy and kept a book propped before her as her fingers flew in needlework.

"I have no desire to see England," she said one evening as the three of them read by smoky lantern light. "Much as I have heard of its wonders, I love the islands and this life. If we need anything English, we just purchase it from a ship."

Aye, Johnny thought. *I could be perfectly happy here, and Claire is an intelligent, pretty-enough girl. Mr. Pocket is kinder than a father.* What more could he ask?

"What's that you're making?" he asked.

"This is a special charm," Claire said softly, holding up a beaded piece of leather. "Half of it I will put in a hollow tree, and the other half I will wear around my neck."

"Why?"

She bent her dark head over her sewing. "I can't tell you."

Johnny guessed. "Claire, where are your parents?"

"They are both dead. My father was an English sailor. My mother was part Ashanti. I am mostly English, I guess."

"Johnny," Mr. Pocket said, looking over his accounts. "Tomorrow I'd like you to take Charles and go along the Kittam River and pick up supplies from a Mr. Oliver Ben. I have a letter from him asking for animal skins, and he will pay you in cotton cloth and other things I need."

"One hundred miles?" Johnny looked surprised. "Sir, I'm not that familiar with the river you mention—."

"Charles is an excellent guide," Mr. Pocket explained. "Take a few extra pounds, Johnny, and buy Claire some gewgaws that girls like."

Claire flushed in happy surprise, and Johnny thought she was as pretty as one of the big tan and rose apricot flowers in her garden.

The morning they left, she cooked a special breakfast, then coming close to him, slipped a cord around his neck, with the beaded pouch hanging on it. "For luck," she whispered. "Wear it until you come back, to protect you."

Johnny laughed and covered it with his shirt, but he felt a keen disappointment at leaving her.

He and Charles, another white man, sailed Mr. Pocket's boat north along the coast toward the Benanoe Islands, where Johnny first landed when he deserted the ship. The rainy season was over, and the weather was hot and dry again.

" 'Tis passing strange the master would send us to Kittam," said Charles. He was a red-haired ex-sailor, tattooed all over his body. "He has not had contact with Oliver Ben for two years. Strange, indeed, that a letter would even arrive from old Ben."

They sailed into the Kittam River, found Oliver Ben, completed their business, and started homeward. Charles suddenly said, "Let's stop at the Plantane Islands, the big one. I have a hunch a ship will come by, and I can trade for the tobacco I need."

Johnny swung the tiller around. "I didn't know a ship would stop at a deserted spot like this."

"Stay on board. I'll walk along the beach a bit."

Johnny watched him lower the canoe overboard and paddle to shore. He dropped anchor and watched Charles through his telescope. Strange it was that Charles thought a ship would stop at this remote place.

Suddenly he saw Charles run around, gathering driftwood and sticks, light a fire with his flint, cover it with a wet bit of canvas, to make a smoke signal. Turning his telescope to sea, Johnny saw a ship.

His first thought was fear, the next thought that Charles was up to no good. The ship kept going; then it stopped and dropped anchor. Charles rammed the canoe through the surf, paddled furiously, and reached the ship's side. A rope ladder was lowered, and he climbed aboard.

Strange. Very strange. Johnny waited impatiently. Had they been a half hour later, they would have missed the ship. What ship was it? Where was she bound? What was Charles thinking about, to stop a ship just for tobacco for himself?

Charles came back in another half hour, climbed aboard, hauled up the canoe, and began to stutter his excitement. "J-Johnny, it's you—*you*—they're looking for! No, not for deserting. Your father! Your father paid the captain to look for you! You must go back with him, he said. A distant relative has died and left you some money! The captain has orders to redeem you, even if it costs half of his cargo! Johnny, there's your chance to get away from here! Africa is the white man's grave, Johnny. You see how Burt Langerman is? Johnny, something made me stop here and notice that ship. Do you believe in Divine Providence?"

Johnny was stunned, torn two ways. What need had he of England now, or his father, or of ransom? Charles just wanted him away so he would have his job. And Claire? Yes, Charles wanted Claire.

Polly—all the memories rushed back over him in a flood. Polly, the little beauty, his darling, he had never really forgotten her. If there was the slightest chance . . . if he had an income they could marry. . . .

"You are telling me true?" he demanded of Charles.

Charles pointed out to sea. The ship's longboat was halfway to shore, and in it was the captain himself.

"Coming to plead with you," Charles said. "Hurry, get ashore and greet him proper."

Johnny swung himself down into the canoe and beached at a wharf where traders met. The longboat sent out a canoe, and the captain and two men came ashore.

"Captain Bigalow, sir. I'm looking for one John Newton, of Liverpool, lately of the ship H.M.S. *Harwich*."

John held out his hand to the other. "I'm John Newton, captain."

"Your father is very desirous of seeing you return to England. His friend, Mr. Joseph Manesty, owner of the ship, commissioned me to find you at any cost. Further, a relative of yours died and left you a nice income. If you will return with me, you will be fed at my table and lodge in my cabin, be my companion without any work expected of you."

Johnny looked slowly from the captain to Charles, hardly able to believe what he was hearing. Polly—would she be waiting?

"Aye, I'll go with you," he said. And to Charles. "I want nothing I left behind. You're welcome to it. Here," he slid the cord of Claire's charm over his head and put it around Charles' neck. "You keep this, and may it bring you all you hope for."

10

Rescued!

February, 1747. The ship, *Newcomer*, was a merchantman trading for gold; ivory; beeswax; and dyers' wood, from which colors were obtained. It took many months of searching to collect such a cargo. The *Newcomer* had already been trading along the coast of Africa for four months, beginning at Gambia. The valuable wood was not easy to find.

The captain traded glass beads and yards of scarlet cloth to the Temne chiefs in return for gold and ivory, cheating them of any fair profit.

Johnny's first thought was to ask if an able seaman, Austin Handwick, was aboard. He found Steenie helping shift ballast in the hold.

"Johnny Newton!" Steenie's grimy bulldog face lit up, and he seized his friend's arm. "Gave you up for dead, blamed if I didn't. Aye, I got a bellyful of slaving, so I signed on an honest ship."

"Have you heard the news? I've inherited a nice sum of money and as soon as we get home—."

"Miss Polly will wed a sailor," Steenie interrupted with a grin.

"No sailor! I'll set myself up in business, I will! Steenie, advise me. If you were a young man with prospects, what would you do? Open a countinghouse? Go into law? Trade? Command a ship?" Johnny strutted back and forth so his friend could note the cut of his clothes.

"Wouldn't ye miss the sea?"

Johnny mulled it over. Would he really like living in a house ashore, where every day was the same? Walking to work, sitting at a desk until the clock told the quitting hour, walking home? The next day starting out all over again?

"We wouldn't have to live in England," he said. "I could take the object of my affections to Jamaica or Spain. I'd buy a plantation and grow fruit—with a little herb garden for Polly. Come, Steenie, quit work and let's celebrate. Call some of your friends and go with me to the purser and we'll ask extra rations of food and grog. I'll have the cook boil us a pudding with spices and sugar, tied up in a cloth."

"You'll be hung afore the day's over!" Steenie admired.

"My good man, I dine with the captain, I sleep in his cabin, I am a gentleman of leisure now. Surely I can entertain a few friends."

Steenie finished hauling bales of cloth in a wheelbarrow. "To think I've lived to see such a day!" he marveled. "I'm happy for ye, Johnny-lad."

"Steenie, come work for me, when I get established!" Johnny's eyes shone at the thought of helping his faithful friend.

"Me? Wot am I fit for but the sea?"

"You can work, laboring like other men. I don't mean you need to keep books or accounts or anything like that. Steenie, I'm making you my foreman on the plantation!"

He threw his arms around the old man, and together they went on deck. Steenie introduced him to Rufus and Harvey, old sailors like himself.

The purser, Old Nipcheese, was in his narrow quarters, totting up his accounts. He wore knee breeches, vest, and a shabby coat with tails. The buttons were hanging by threads or missing, since he had given up trying to button his coat over his vast middle. His fondness for cheese and for stealing from the larder earned him the nickname.

"Dinner for four, and put it on my account," Johnny said boldly. Old Nipcheese glared at him through little, rimless spectacles. "I'll be asking the captain about that." He trotted away and returned looking sour and disappointed.

"Dinner for four," Johnny repeated, and the purser grudgingly signed a note for the cook. "And a platter of bread and cheese for the purser, along with some wine," Johnny added slyly. Old Nipcheese's lumpy face brightened, "Yes, *sir!*"

"To pinch poor men's bellies is a great piece of villainy," Rufus grumbled under his breath about the purser. "We never get anything extra from that penny pincher."

"You will, now that I'm here," Johnny boasted. "I've inherited money, and I'm going to buy me a plantation on an island, and Steenie will work for me." In an explosion of goodwill he added, "And you, too, Rufus and Harvey, come along with us. Better than getting knocked about on a ship."

Rufus hitched up the rope that anchored his breeches in place. "She's my woman," he said of the ship, "and I'm wedded to her, and I love her. Thank ye kindly, but I could never turn my back on her while she's afloat."

"I'll go," said white-haired Harvey. "I'd rather be in Turkish slavery than this here life."

The four of them sat alone at the midshipmen's mess table, and the cook brought the food to them. Johnny planned it that way so it would seem like a party. Real coffee, tough and stringy lumps of beef floating in hot gravy, boiled eggs, biscuits, and a suet pudding.

"Your health!" the three cried, clinking tin cups with Johnny.

"Here's to the plantation!" sang out Steenie, "and the trees and the warm sun—and the girl!"

Polly! Within six months he would see her, all his dreams come true. He wanted to save his gentleman's clothes, so after the feast he and the other three men picked out clothes from the slop chest. "Put it all to my account," Johny said grandly. He folded the clothes Mr. Pocket had given him and locked them away in his sea chest.

He felt more comfortable in sailor's knee breeches and striped shirt and cotton cap. Steenie helped himself to three yards of bright yellow flowered cloth. "Always did fancy sewing myself a shirt," he said. Rufus and Harvey sported new caps, belts, and canvas coats for rainy weather.

"You needn't report for duty yet. Let's sit on deck and yarn. A prize for the one who tells the most awful story. True, mind you."

A half dozen other men joined them in the shade of the mast, and Steenie began. "This here's just a bit of news. After you left the *Harwich*, Johnny, news was passed aboard that the ship *Dundee*, a-whaling up north, found a man froze dead in a block of ice."

"Aye, that happens," said Johnny.

"Wait!" Steenie leaned forward knocking his pipe against the mast. "The coin in his pocket was dated fourteen eighty-four!"

The men sat in awed silence, until Harvey spoke up. "Shipped out three years ago around the Horn and sat in the Doldrums six weeks, praying for a breath of wind. Scraped barnacles from the sides of the ship to eat. The first man died. Some of the others ate him. I didn't have the heart for that sort of thing. Then the scurvy began. Lost half my teeth, pains in my head, roof of my mouth like raw meat. Me legs swelled like trees, funny spots all over me. Some of the men sprung running ulcers and rotten bones. One man who broke an arm twenty years before had the healed bone come apart in two pieces. Some that was most cheerful and healthy in bed got up to work the pumps and dropped dead after two steps.

"The sails slatting against the masts day and night wore them to shreds and wore our nerves to shreds. Captain made us take off our clothes and make sails of them. Strung up all the hammocks on the yards for sails. Not a breeze. More men dropped dead without a word."

Harvey stared off into the distance, and finally a man said, "You—ate—too?"

"I ate," said Harvey in a dull tone.

Rufus hastened to change the subject. "What I have to tell ain't horrible, just interestin'. You mind that in seventeen nineteen the *Albany* and the *Discovery* set out from England with Captain James Knight? Ain't been heard of since. Twenty-eight years."

"Poor devils."

Johnny stretched out his legs and reclined on one bent arm. "Two years ago Parliament put up a reward of twenty thousand pounds for a captain to discover a passage from Hudson Bay to the Pacific. Steenie, that's it! We'll outfit a ship, small whaler with fifteen men, and go in search of a passage. And if we catch a whale or two along the way, why the government pays a bounty on them!"

"I have a true tale," said one sailor hoarsely. "Still gives me the horrors."

"Tell! Tell!" the men clamored.

"A ship was being built in the docks at Liverpool one year and was nigh on to being finished when a drunken carpenter was pushed into the hold and boarded up by a man, Eppy, who stole his tools. We shipped out, ran into rocks, and she sank at sea. We was all saved and put aboard another, but one night we saw the ghost ship. She tried to ram us broadside, and we on deck felt it slide over us like a wraith. There was only a chill and a dampish smell and an emptiness in our brains. We saw it again, a week later. The ghost ship, piloted by the dead carpenter, was following the man what did the murder. The murderer quit the sea and took a land job. He thought to get away. The ship sailed over the land at him one night, and he tried to hang hisself."

"How do you know—?" Johnny began, then horror clipped his tongue. "Your name?"

"Yes. Eppy." The man was skeleton-thin and hollow-eyed. His hands shook all the time. "Sometimes I still see it. Sometimes I feel the clammy, foggy hands of the dead man on my neck."

"More drink!" Harvey roared to break the spell. "Have a snootful, lads! Come, drink to Johnny and good luck!"

Steenie stood up and lifted his hand for silence. "While we're all together-like, jolly good friends and all, I want to ask—I want to say—well I mean to say thank-you to the Almighty that our Johnny has finally come into good fortune, for Lord knows this lad—."

"Stow it!" Johnny hissed, but he felt secretly pleased. Steenie should have been his father, so kind and thoughtful he was. He couldn't be getting angry at anything right now.

"So I think a prayer is in order. Men, would you respectfully rise?" The fellows dragged themselves upright, a few grumbling under their breath about "too hot for prayers," and, " 'tisn't even Sunday, blast him."

Steenie pulled a little black book out of his shirt and read the Prayer of Thanks from the Established Church of England prayer book. "Don't sit, yet," he said. "I want to tell you true out of the Holy Book that oncet another boy like Johnny shipped off to a far country and was a-wastin' of his poor father's money—."

"Never had none from my father!" Johnny declared hotly.

"No, you didn't. But you was a-wastin' of your life and had many a danger, many a fright, many a hard adventure, but all the time you had a father what loved you and offered a ransom—."

"Fine way he showed love sometimes," Johnny snorted.

"Well, some fathers don't know how to show it. But many a time he bailed you out o' trouble, and he was a-thinkin' of you all the time, and now he's sent for you to come and be forgiven—."

"*Forgiven?*" Johnny stamped one foot. "Steenie, begging your pardon and all, might we sit down on deck? Aye, 'tis too hot to stand at attention, and your story is too long."

"Oh, I'm about finished," Steenie said. "This here is Holy Bible truth. All a man need do is say, 'Father, I have sinned.' " He hurried on. "Our blessed Saviour bore our sins on Hisself so's we could receive heaven—."

"Mr. Handwick!" Captain Bigalow stood in the sail shadows. "Mr. Handwick, preaching of any kind, except by an ordained minister of the Church, is forbidden by law. Gathering to listen is forbidden. You all could be arrested, every man jack of you, and thrown into prison when we land. But," he looked around at the frightened men, "since this is a special occasion of rejoicing, I will overlook it this time. However I forbid any of you to meet together on this ship for the purpose of discussing religion. Religion is not for seamen—makes them soft. Prayers read on Sunday are sufficient." He turned on his shiny boot heel and stalked away.

The men sprawled back down on the deck. "Are you really a rich man, now, Johnny?" asked one sailor.

"I've come into a bit of money," Johnny said modestly.

"Best to leave this life," the man said. "I've been out on four voyages in seven years and not seen a crooked pence yet. The first ship company went bankrupt afore I got back. I waited three months in Plymouth for another ship, and all the time the landlady of the boarding house kept wanting money. What was I to do? She never stopped complaining and threatening me with debtor's prison, 'til I made out a will in her favor. Then out I ship again without even saying good-bye to my little chickens and poor biddy. They had not the fare to come and see me off. Back I come after two years and got my pay ticket, then sold it at a great loss so I'd have food. My little chickens would starve, save that my biddy is walking the streets to earn money."

"A shame," murmured another man. "A mockery of Magna Charta, that's what it is. A sailor has no rights, lower than a mongrel of the streets."

"I knows a lad what drowned at sea, and his missus never was told of it until three years later," spoke another.

"I knows a seaman waited his pay for twelve years."

"Party's over," Johnny announced abruptly. "We'll have another at journey's end." It had just occurred to him that he hadn't yet seen his father's letter asking him to come home.

Captain Bigalow was in his cabin, following the course of the ship by watching the compass on his desk. Charts and log book lay piled to one side.

"Johnny, do you understand the mathematical systems of the computation of latitude and longitude and distance without landmarks?"

"Yes, sir, I taught myself quite a bit by reading. And I was schooled in math when quite young."

"A good lad. You'll be a help to me on this voyage, for we're venturing another thousand miles south to Cape Lopez."

"Sir!" Johnny said. "I understood we were going straight-away back to England!"

"Still have cargo room," replied the captain.

"But—," Johnny calculated swiftly in his head. "At Cape Lopez we'll be seven thousand miles from home!"

"Aye, about that, counting all the twists and turns and tacking and wearing to catch the trade winds."

Johnny swallowed his disappointment. "Captain, sir, may I see my father's letter?"

"Letter?" Captain Bigalow rubbed his ear. His face was clean-shaven and his hair clipped short. On the desk lay a curly white wig. "Now that I recollect, the packet of letters was left behind."

Johnny's heart sank. "Sir—may I ask—where?"

The captain laughed a little and raised his eyebrows. "Lad, there is no letter—not written down, mind you—but as I live and breathe your father does want you home, and Mr. Manesty, ship's owner, charged me to find you no matter what it cost. Thinks highly of your father, don't you see, and for that you should be grateful—."

Johnny licked lips dry as crumbs and whispered, "And the relative who died and left me money?"

"Now look here, have I asked you to lend a hand aloft? Haven't I treated your friends to food and drink and over-looked misbehavior? Don't you have the run of the ship—a young boy only, not even a midshipman?"

"Captain Bigalow . . . there is no small fortune left me?"

The captain looked down at his gleaming boots as though they entertained him. "Now, lad, I had to say something to get you aboard, as Mr. Manesty ordered me. I could see you were satisfied with your life on the island, native girls and what not—."

"Captain . . . ," Johnny still couldn't believe he'd been tricked. "Captain, sir, do you mean a relative of mine did not die, that I am penniless, in debt to the purser?"

His rising voice alarmed the captain. "Yes, sir, Mr. Newton, that's what I mean! I'm sorry it had to be done that way. Now go off, like a good lad, read the books on my shelf, improve yourself. Be glad your father was good enough—."

Johnny didn't hear any more, for he flung himself out of the cabin, lest he murder the man in cold blood. He was worse off than before! If he'd stayed on the island with Mr. Pocket, in two years he would have been a rich man!

He ran across the deck like a whirlwind, thirsting for a fight, and jumped the entire length of steps into the fo'c'sle, laming one leg and skinning his feet. Steenie grabbed his arm. "Lad, you look like the seven devils! What happened?"

Johnny, in his fury, slammed his balled-up fist into the wooden wall, breaking some fingers and leaving a bloodstain. Seizing a hammock, he ripped it down and began to tear it with his teeth.

"Lord help us!" Steenie fell into the nearest hammock. "For heaven's sake, Johnny, stop! Stop! Rufus! Help! Call the captain!"

Johnny let loose a string of oaths and knocked Steenie back into the hammock. Finally he collapsed on the floor, thrashing around, panting and sobbing in rage.

"Johnny, Johnny, it ain't true? All you said?" Steenie knelt beside him and patted his head. "Oh, Johnny-lad, I'm so sorry,

sorry, sorry. The life you've had, the sufferings you've had. Oh, I was so glad when you told me about the girl—and the plantation—and wanting me to live with you. . . ."

Steenie covered his face and began to blubber. "Oh, such misery for a young lad! Oh, the disappointments and heartache this boy has had! Johnny, Johnny, it will be all right. We'll find a way. And we *are* going home to England, lad, that's *something!*"

Johnny lay still and let Steenie bandage his fingers and bring him vittles. After sundown he walked on the deck a while, and most of the men knew enough to let him alone.

He thought it over. He would not be indebted to the captain for anything; he would go aloft in the rigging and work again, four hours on, four off, like the other men.

He thought he would drown in the bitterness welling up from inside him. *Polly, Polly.* Again, only the thought of her kept him from killing himself and having done with all his troubles.

One man, who hadn't heard of his disappointment, stopped to talk. "Say, matey, you said we should all tell the awfullest story we knew, but you didn't tell one."

Johnny shrugged and passed him by. *Aye,* he thought, *and my story is the awfullest of all.*

11

Dancing With Death

As the ship continued on a southerly course, life fell into the same routine day and night. At seven bells in the morning the bosun piped all hands awake. Each man unhooked his hammock, rolled it up, and stowed it around the bulwark on deck to make more room.

Sailors took turns, working in teams, swabbing down the deck with buckets of seawater. Anyone who lingered in his hammock was awakened by icy water, leaking through cracks in the planks of the deck and down onto his head.

At eight bells breakfast was served to all: bean soup, flour biscuits hard as wood, water. Twice a week the between decks were cleaned out and hosed down.

Repair of the running rigging was a never-ending job. Masts needed to be sluiced with grease. Sails were mended and patched.

Men off duty lay on deck, under a canvas awning, almost suffocated by the humid climate, staring at a vacant, dreamy sea. During brief showers, they used the awning to catch drinking water.

One day the shout "ship, ho!" broke the monotony, and
Johnny hung over the rail with the others to see what would
happen. The other ship sent out its boat and offered to trade
fresh fish for desperately needed drinking water. Captain Bigalow agreed, and the boat returned overflowing with nets of
fish, some still alive and struggling.

In the bow of the small boat Johnny spotted a mound of colored rags, a long nose, and a red and white striped nightcap
drooping down over it. The figure appeared to be tangled in
the limp arms of a dead octopus.

"Lend me your telescope!" He snatched the instrument from
Steenie and looked long and hard. He swore and smacked
Steenie on the back.

"Take a look! Gut me if it ain't Old Burgoo!"

"Oh my sweet dollies, a royal welcome for Old Burgoo! And
haven't I been a-slavin' over a fishy stove night and day, day
and night, for that rascally crew! Fish for breakfast, fish for
dinner, fish for supper, fish stew, fish baked, fish broiled, fish
boiled, fish chowder, stuffed fish, steamed fish, filet of fish, fish
with rice dressing, fish sauce. . . ." He drew a shuddering
breath. "Then there was pickled smelts, lobster, cod, eels,
flounder, scallops, bass, shad, salmon. Hanged afore I go back
to a fishin' ship, and Old Burgoo is so glad to see 'is friends
again. . . ."

"You unwashed heathen, you!" Steenie gave Burgoo a bear
hug, and Johnny delightedly shook Burgoo's smelly hand.

"Hooroar, lads, we're together ag'in!" Old Burgoo clapped
his hands and danced a crooked jig. "Oh, I'll smell o' the deep
for a day or two, couldn't get that blamed eight-legged thing to
stop a-huggin' o' me, but he'll be in the soup for them lads,
may they perish to a watery grave!"

Burgoo fumbled inside his tattered shirt and produced a wa-
terproof bag. "Here's letters, my bullies, three for our
Johnny, from Kent, and I won't say the young lady's name, for
it's no man's business—."

"Give them here!" Johnny snatched the bag. "Skip, now, Burgoo, do, and get cleaned of that smell, and get some clothes from the purser. Put it to my account. Your head's lousy as a cuckoo."

"How did they let you get off that ship?" Steenie demanded.

"Gave up my pay ticket," said Burgoo. "And, don't peach, but, he dropped his voice, "at last night's supper a score of men took sick of the fish stew, prayin' to die, and the cap'n he says, 'Burgoo, I'll put you on the next ship we meet, if I don't throw you to the sharks first.' So here I am, and trim my ears if I ain't happy to be relieved o' them pirates!"

Johnny went off by himself to read the letters from Polly. They were written one month apart. "Dear John...." *Dear!* She loved him, then, "We all read your letter...." *She* read his letter! He sniffed it and thought the smell of kitchen spices still clung to it, or English daisies and harebells and new-mown hay. "England is so cold now, and we wonder how you are." Polly, thinking of him all the time! "I wrote some poetry, and mother said it was not too bad." She wrote poetry about him! "Catherine and I made cherry tarts one day." She was learning to cook! What could it mean, except that she was thinking of soon keeping her own home? "I pray for our seamen every night." Polly *prayed* for him! He laid aside his rejection of God for a moment and pictured her in a flannel robe, kneeling by her bedside.

"We are glad to hear you are in business and look forward to seeing you on your return to England."

Polly was *waiting* for him!

"What are you grinning about? It's running all over your face." Steenie joked, passing by.

"Nothing." Johnny folded the letters and wore them next to his heart. It eased him a little to know she wasn't wed.

The ship continued down toward Cape Lopez. The crew had been without fresh fruit, and one day Johnny felt his jaw ache. The dreaded scurvy! The ship's carpenter offered to pull his teeth. Johnny lay down on the wooden workbench, and the carpenter tapped each tooth sharply with a metal spoon until Johnny yelped, "That's the one!"

A side tooth. He'd never miss it, the carpenter assured him. Only took a minute to put his head in a wooden vise and hold still. The carpenter eagerly flourished a pair of pincers, there was a spurt of blood, and, "Drawn out!" shouted the man.

Johnny rinsed his mouth with salt water and spit over the side. He felt better already. Scurvy was caused by lack of exercise, the mates always said. That kept the men from shirking.

Every evening at dusk the drummer boy beat a rolling tattoo, and all lights were put out, even pipes. Fire at sea was a fear they all lived with, for there was no hope of controlling it. Johnny tried sneaking a pipe one evening, when the watch cried six bells, but three men with buckets rushed up and doused the water over his head.

He bunked with the other hands before the mast and avoided the captain. At first he worked on deck, hoisting the mainsail each day. Five ancient riggers helped, bracing their feet against the mast, two hauling on the rope, the other three using all their strength to fasten the end of the arm-thick rope to a belaying pin.

The first mate noticed his skill and asked if he wanted to go aloft. Johnny shrugged, agreed, and actually was glad to be working. Time might pass quicker, but he knew it would be a year before they saw England.

The hot weather flagged down the men's spirits, made them short-tempered, bored, restless.

One evening Johnny lolled on deck with Steenie, Old Burgoo, Rufus, and Harvey. Old Burgoo, mousing around in the hold, found them a small cask of rum and one of Holland gin. They kept it covered with a piece of sail. Rufus found a large seashell for a glass. Johnny had an idea.

"We'll not just sip at it a little now and a little tomorrow night," he said. "We'll hold a contest! Each man drinks a shell full of rum and one of gin, until we see bottom! A prize for the man who holds out the longest!"

"I don't like it," Steenie said bluntly.

"*I* likes it," said Burgoo. Rufus and Harvey agreed.

"I'll start, and I'll propose the first toast," Johnny insisted. He thought a minute. "A curse on the man who takes the first drink, and may his soul go to the devil!"

He tipped up the shell and loudly pronounced his own doom. Steenie took a swig. "To England," he said glumly. "May we get home soon."

"To England!" shouted the others, passing around the shell.

Johnny felt his brain take fire, and he marveled at how clever he suddenly sounded. "To Lucifer!" he said loudly. "Aye, I'll follow him to the end of the earth!"

The other men didn't respond. "You got the backbone of a wet piece of hemp!" Johnny spat at them. He poured the liquor into him and began to blaspheme God. Not content with repeating sailor talk, he began to mock the Trinity, going into great detail, wilder and wilder.

"I don't like this," Steenie said suddenly, and lumbered to his feet. "You'll bring God's wrath on this ship with such talk. My head is thumpin' already from that mixture."

"May the wrath come on me!" Johnny filled up the shell from both casks and gobbled down the stinging drink. "May I be doomed, burn on the coals, may my soul be lost forever!" His head spun like a top, and he didn't care what he said.

"I'm a-goin' to bed," Steenie announced. "Johnny, you've said too much, and you're full o' an evil spirit. I'm feared to stay in your company."

Johnny felt a tiger in his brain, gnawing and clawing, and he got up and began to dance around the deck, cursing God, shaking his fists at heaven, and emptying out all his hate to the sky.

Rufus and Harvey nodded against the mast, too dazed to move. Steenie went below, and only Old Burgoo lingered.

"Sing o' the maypole and midsummer night . . . ," Johnny sang at the top of his lungs, dancing in circles, stomping his heels, making high jumps, hands on hips. "The Bible is a jolly Book. . . ." He poked fun at the Gospel, the creed, the prayers, and began again on deity.

The little cook had to shout to be heard, following Johnny around as he danced. "Old Burgoo's never heered such talk, not from the worst! Come to bed, Johnny, I'm feared to leave you alone, for you're a devil if ever I seed a devil. I had a matey, oncet, mixed gin and rum and hung hisself with his own garters."

Johnny choked, laughing, and spun around and around like a dust ball. A small breeze lifted his cotton cap and sent it sailing over the edge of the ship. "Launch the jolly boat, I'm coming!" he shouted and flung himself against the bulwark. Climbing up on the rail, he was ready to jump when Burgoo caught his ankle. With a yell and a curse, Johnny fell backward onto the deck.

Old Burgoo leaned over him, gasping for breath, and sat on his chest. "You young devil, it ain't the jolly boat, it's the shadder of the mast, you young fool. All the ship is a-bed and them two drunk, and who'd you think would fish you out of the briny? You're a-dancin' with death, you are! They's sharks about tonight, you imp of Satan, and poor Old Burgoo wot got no strength in his arms kept you from goin' to the evil one, I did. Now if you move, I'll cut your throat!"

The next thing Johnny knew was a torrent of water sloshed across his face from a bucket and Old Burgoo climbing back on his chest to hold him down.

"I won't be bullied—," he began, then the masts above him seemed to waver, and he thought his head rolled off and across the deck. He went unconscious for the rest of the night.

That week a plague of illness hit the crew, and Johnny woke up one morning feeling as though he had been keelhauled. He was feverish and chilly at the same time. His head hurt, and his stomach heaved. He visited the privy every few minutes, swaying as he walked.

"Report to sick berth," Steenie urged, but Johnny shook his head.

Old Burgoo stopped by when he could. "A bit of honey and tar for the coughs." He urged a bottle of thick, black stuff on him. "Take a nip now and then."

"Don't have the coughs," mumbled Johnny.

"Take some anyhow," Burgoo said. "Prevents the coughs."

Steenie called the first mate, and when he saw how sick Johnny was, he ordered two men to carry him to the sick berth. Johnny lay in a crowded row of hammocks and hardly knew it when the ship's doctor bled him, taking twelve ounces of blood from his arm. The doctor ordered quinine for the fever, but so many were sick that two days went by before he could return to check on Johnny.

By that time, ten men had died, and Johnny could smell death in the air. Steenie offered to take care of him and gave him the medicine and sips of water.

Old Burgoo sneaked him soup, but Johnny was too sick to eat. "One of them there African diseases blown off the coast at us," was Burgoo's opinion. "I swares Creaky Joints don't know wot he's a-doin', bleedin' every last soul, whether they got the bloody flux or not."

Steenie sat by him and fanned him with a piece of paper every spare minute he could steal from work. Once he said in a guarded voice, "Johnny, don't think I'm preaching again, but suppose you die? Johnny-lad, suppose you die without making peace with God?"

Johnny twisted his head from side to side, trying to ease the pain. He didn't answer.

"I'm praying for you, not aloud, for it's forbidden, but in my soul, Johnny, I'm praying."

That night the doctor called Steenie aside and said, "That one is going soon. Has he last words or affairs to settle?"

"Johnny Newton?"

"Aye, him and another four or five. I'd advise you, Mr. Handwick, to stay clear of the sick ones, lest you take it."

"I'll nurse Johnny to the end!" Steenie declared. "I'm sound as a horse."

Johnny didn't die, though he didn't care one way or the other. The worst seemed over, and he could drink water and drank all he could hold. The plague departed as quickly as it had struck. By the time he was back to work, the dead men had been buried and the ship approached the equator.

"You ever crossed the Line?" Rufus asked.

"My first time," Johnny said. "I suppose I get keelhauled?"

"None of that. Not allowed anymore. I shan't tell you what'll happen to you."

"My thanks, I'm favored," Johnny laughed. "The worst would be a pleasure, compared to the sickness I've had."

Johnny held his sextant to his eye, squinted through the telescope, and adjusted a little mirror until the sun's image seemed to sit on the horizon. The ship rolled to starboard, the sun jiggled up and down, and he had to begin over.

"Right you are," he said. "Almost to the equator."

In the dogwatch of late afternoon, the men were piped on deck and seated in a circle. Johnny and two others who never crossed the Line were asked to stand. Over the side of the ship climbed Old Burgoo, to the roll of a drum, dressed as King Neptune, god of the sea. Robed in green, he carried a sort of pitchfork the carpenter had designed, with a fish stuck on its point.

A wooden throne painted gold was set up on the midship hatch, and Old Burgoo hopped atop and stuck a crown made of tin spoons tied together on top of his head.

"Ahoy, me faithful subjects, England's best, true blue hearts of oak, good King Neptune welcomes the green sticks wot never crossed the Line, the three innercent babes—"

"Aw, get on with it!"

"Sluice 'im off!"

"And since we knows fine words butter no parsnips, Old Burgoo will now ask 'is jolly mates to step up and begin the frolic."

Two sailors seized the three "innercents" and slathered a slimy green mixture all over them, then shaved their heads with a frightful razor. Ropes were tied around their waists, and they were thrown overboard and rinsed off.

Johnny came up sputtering and blowing water out of his mouth and nose and was allowed to sit on the deck by Neptune's throne. The mate broke out an extra grog ration and passed around burned biscuits along with sticks of tobacco. Steenie offered his tinderbox so the men could smoke.

Some of the seamen put on a skit, making fun of a sailor's life. When it was over, Burgoo dragged a sea chest up on deck and, throwing back the lid, revealed a lady's wardrobe—long skirts, shawls, bonnets, aprons and stockings.

"A weddin' dowery was put a-board by mistake," he said, when the laughter died down. "Seein' our three innercents are now wedded to the sea, it's fittin' we have a weddin' party."

The men whooped with pleasure and began to dress in the finery. The fiddler struck up a lively tune, and the men, some in shawls, some in dresses on backwards, bonnets over tarry pigtails, skipped in a circle, flipped imaginary fans, flirted, and simpered.

Johnny laughed until tears bubbled from his eyes. Old Burgoo kept his dignity as king with great difficulty and his foot tapped and his head bobbed as he longed to join in the fun.

Johnny looked around for Steenie and missed him. He wasn't on deck and he wasn't aloft or in the galley, so Johnny went below and found him in bed, one hand clutching his forehead.

"Came over me all on a sudden," he whimpered. "I feel so sick, so hot, but me feets are icy cold." He broke off as a chill overtook him, and he shuddered and rattled in his bunk. He was sick over the edge, and Johnny brought him a slop bucket. He took the extra cotton blanket from his sea chest and wrapped it around Steenie.

"You took the plague a little late." He tried to make light of it, but he felt a little fearful. Steenie was older; he might get really sick.

"You should be in the sick berth," he said, but Steenie pleaded with him. "Men go there to die," he moaned. "No air. I never thought it was good for sick men not to have air."

"Can you take a little water?"

Steenie groaned and shook his head. "Nothin' now, I'm spinnin' around like a whirly-gig, lad. Let me try to sleep."

Johnny climbed up on deck and called Rufus and Old Burgoo. "He's got to take 'is medicine," said Old Burgoo. "I'll fetch it."

He returned with quinine and the doctor's permission for Steenie to stay in his own bed.

Johnny sat by him his four hours off duty. Steenie's neck and face turned bright red and the doctor bled him twice, but Steenie was not aware. His breathing was labored, and every once in a while he skipped a breath. For the first time Johnny thought of Steenie dying. *No, no, how could such a thing be?* he cried silently. *Not Steenie.* How would he manage without Steenie? Steenie was the damper for his fire. Steenie was the calm after his storms.

"He took sick taking care of me," Johnny said aloud, and his face crumpled. "He'd never have caught it if he hadn't hung over me all the time."

Steenie opened his eyes at the sound of a voice. "Johnny-lad, are you there?" he said weakly. "Johnny—say a prayer for me, for I'm goin'."

Going? No! What kind of prayer? Johnny jumped up and rummaged desperately in his sea chest. No books there. He slipped the string with its key off Steenie's neck and searched his sea chest. The prayer book was gone.

"Wait! Steenie, hold on! I'll find a prayer!" Johnny ran to fetch Old Burgoo, and they found the mate, who found the captain, who had been napping.

"A prayer? There's Prayers for the Dead in the book," the captain complained. "Are you needing that?"

"No, you villain!" Johnny yelled, almost out of his head with grief. "A prayer for the sick, you turnip head! Come say a prayer for Steenie!"

"Take care!" The mate pulled him away. "Don't speak that way to the captain."

Johnny began to cry. "*You* come say a prayer!" He seized the mate's arm. "Hurry, it's for Steenie!"

The mate pulled himself loose. "Mr. Newton! Control yourself. It's not allowed."

Johnny ran back to Steenie, knelt by him, put his arms around the big, shaggy head, and pulled it on to his shoulder. "Steenie," he sobbed, "You don't need a prayer, you'll be all right, you'll work on the plantation with me and Polly. . . ."

Rufus gently untangled Johnny's arms. "He's all right, now, Johnny, can't you see? Come away, now."

In the morning the crew assembled on deck and prayers were read. Steenie's body, sewed up in his hammock and weighed down with shot, was lowered into the sea.

"We commit the body of Austin Handwick to the deep, and his soul to the mercy of Almighty God," droned the captain.

Johnny stood at attention with the others, but he felt dead inside, as though he had slipped over the edge with Steenie and only his shell stood on deck.

Old Burgoo looked at him mournfully. "He was your conscience," he said, "and now he's gone."

12

Quicksand!

December, 1747. The crew of the *Newcomer* was as dried out and brittle as the salt pork they gnawed. The drinking water was yellow and scummy and the biscuits full of rat droppings. Tropical heat lay like a cloak over the ship.

"We all need fresh meat," the mate, Pearce, said one day to Johnny and Rufus as the ship approached the southern tip of Africa. "Johnny, you've lived in Africa; will you take a few of the men ashore to hunt?"

"I didn't go inland—save once," Johnny protested, "and it wasn't to hunt."

"Captain says we need fresh meat," Pearce repeated stubbornly. He was a man with thick neck and arms and powerful muscles. He'd captained a ship that foundered, and nobody would hire him since that time.

"We could hunt us a Christmas dinner," said Rufus eagerly. "I'll go."

Old Burgoo hobbled by, dragging a bag of spoiled onions. He cocked his ears, then began to sing:

"Oh, Christmas is a-creepin' up on the sly,
And Old Burgoo fancies an elephant pie;
Some tiger paws for presents, a coconut for me,
And a monkey's tail to hang on the jolly tree."

"Hold your tongue," snapped Johnny, "unless you're willing to come along."

Old Burgoo's pop eyes bulged out of his head. "Go ashore? In a heathen land? Shall I? Shall I? Shilly-shally. Oh, no, matey, Old Burgoo must stay with the solid deck under 'is poor old feet and fix you up a flavorish gravy for the meat. Oh, we'll have a jolly Christmas dinner if you fetch us a tiger or two." He jiggled his cracked and blackened feet in a dance step. "Oh, mateys, wot a feast! O' course if you don't go, we'll have some more fish—fried fish, boiled fish—."

"We'll go," said Johnny hastily. "Rufus and I and Harvey. Who else? Alfred?"

Alfred was a fifteen-year-old, an orphan whose father had died in debtor's prison.

"Yes, take Alfred," said the mate. "We'll anchor off Cape Lopez, and maybe you can find fruit or berries."

"Nothing at Cape Lopez but jungle." Johnny remembered the books he'd read.

"That way you can't desert," Pearce said nastily.

Johnny took a dislike to him and made a mental note to get even. A few days later when the ship anchored, Johnny and the other three men were allowed guns and provisions. When the ship's boat scraped the sandy beach, they weighted the boat with a heavy rock and started into the bush, using a well-worn path.

"Don't ever leave the path, and don't let the sun set on us," Johnny cautioned. He still shivered when he remembered his experience with Burt. "And don't eat anything—could be poisoned. Pearce don't know what he's talking about."

The cool, shaded forest gave them a little relief from the

broiling sun that beat down aboard ship. They stepped slowly, listening for any sound. Deep into the forest the trees closed overhead and the light dimmed. An hour passed without their seeing a living thing except small snakes.

"Stop a bit," Johnny commanded. "This path is so worn I fear the animals must be leary of it. Let's mark this tree and each go a different direction." He notched a sign on the tree with his knife. "Rufus, go straight. Harvey, to the left. I'll go right. Alfred, you're the youngest. Stay by this tree with the water flask."

He looked up, but the sun could no longer be seen. "Notch every tenth tree with your knife. After fifty trees, return to Alfred. Keep an even keel. Be very quiet, and we're sure to see some game."

They started out, and Johnny walked to the right, keeping his steps in a straight line, careful to notch trees. After the first ten trees, he almost turned back. He didn't have much shot with him, and he should have told the others to notch *both sides* of the tree, so they could return quickly.

Breaking down bushes and sweeping vines aside, he kept on for about a half hour. Every once in a while a snake glided soundlessly almost across his feet. Then he heard a shot— two—three—four. One of the men just bagged their Christmas dinner!

He turned to go back, became confused, and stood still. *Fire your gun, you woodenhead,* he told himself. *They'll find you.*

His foot slipped in the squashy mud, and all of a sudden he was knee-deep. *Quicksand,* he thought. *Lie flat, get flat, don't let yourself go straight down.*

He tried to roll onto his side, but slid up to his thighs in mucky water, with no footing. The closest man was one-half hour away! *They'll think I'm shooting game, if I fire.* He loaded the gun and shot upward. Loaded and fired again and again. By this time he was waist deep, his feet being sucked lower and lower.

Cursing and biting his lip, he fired all his shells. He could smell the black, slimy mud that oozed and bubbled. A flock of bright parrots shrieked overhead, and small branches fell around him from the shots.

He reached for a branch as thick as his arm and tried to sit on it. Too late, the cold pull of the muck was dragging him under. Dropping his useless gun, he used his arms to try and push himself higher.

His feet and legs were helpless, pulled by an invisible, greedy tide. He didn't dare struggle. He saved his strength to keep his head up and breathe and hold his arms high. He should have had more shot left. Then he remembered—fool, why hadn't he brought more? Time dragged on, his arms ached, and he knew he was sinking again.

He thought he heard Rufus' voice, then he actually saw him crashing through the brush. "Help!" He managed a feeble sound.

Rufus immediately knew what to do. Ripping down vines, he threw them to Johnny. "Tie them under your armpits, hurry!" he grunted. Working like a frenzied man, he shot down a giant branch and threw it to Johnny. "The others are coming. You left most of your shot behind, so I was bringing it to you. Harvey got us a buffalo or wild cow or some such thing."

Johnny tied the vines under his arms, then grabbed the thick branch. "Lie out flat, now!" Rufus shouted. "Harvey! Hurry on here, we've got to get Johnny out!"

As they pulled, Johnny forced himself to rise a little until he could throw himself flat on his face in the muck, which brought his feet up a little.

"Pull!" Rufus groaned. One vine snapped, but the others held, and Johnny, one arm over the branch, felt the muck give way a little. Alfred ran up, and they all pulled and threw more branches. Ever so slowly Johnny was eased out of the quicksand and pulled free by the men. They wiped him down with leaves, but he smelled like garbage.

"You've had another escape from death," Rufus said, looking at him sideways. "Sets a man back on his heels a bit, don't it?"

"Don't care one way or the other." Johnny tried to scrape the muck from his clothes with a piece of bark. "What did you bag?"

"Wild cow. Good eating. We'll have a feast. Let's start back."

"Not that way!" Johnny corrected him sharply. "Go left."

"Wait." Young Alfred stopped them. "Go right, I remember that swinging patch of flowers."

Rufus shook his head. "Straight, I tell you. Didn't I just come that way?"

Harvey held up his hand. "To be honest, I don't know anymore. I swear the blamed stuff grows back up as soon as we trample it down. Don't move from here until we're certain. Blamed if the sun didn't blot itself out of the sky."

"Let's stay together this time," Johnny said, trembling in spite of himself. "Mark this big cottonwood tree all around, and we'll keep coming back to it. Now let's march straight ahead for one-half hour and notch the trees."

After fifteen minutes of tramping through the bush, they stopped to rest. "Rufus, do you recognize anything?"

"Not a thing."

"Turn back," Johnny said. "We'll try another way."

In a few minutes they came to a trampled crossroads. "Didn't notice this before," Harvey said. "Now which way?"

Johnny was stumped. *Don't let them see you're worried,* he thought. "Rufus and Harvey, go that way. Alfred, come with me. Notch every tree. Go about fifteen minutes, then return and report."

Not long after he heard a yelp from Rufus, so he and Alfred ran back along the trail they'd broken.

"Found the flask Alfred dropped," Rufus told them. "Come along, we're all right now."

In twenty minutes they were back at the cottonwood tree and the animal Harvey bagged. They tied it up with rope, slung it to a branch, and took turns, by twos, carrying it on their shoulders.

"Whew!" Johnny mopped his dripping forehead and face with the rag tied around his head. "Box my ears for a fool if I ever set foot in a jungle again!"

They found the boat waiting, loaded the animal, and reached the ship. Old Burgoo danced in delight as they hauled up the animal.

"Oh, wot a marv'lous lardy meat pie he'll make, my little plum puddings! I'll whittle ye small as chips, me love-a-ly ox, and serve ye up in brown grease with flour dumplin's!"

Christmas Day. The bosun piped all men on deck, and the captain, splendid in uniform and glittering medals, read a holiday message from His Most Gracious Majesty from the prayer book. Old Burgoo kept his word and served up slabs of roast meat, with lots of extras that made every mouth water.

In the dogwatch the men on deck played blindman's buff and frolicked like children. When they tired, the mate suggested they tell of other Christmases.

All the men thought of home and Christmas ashore. "I smelled roast chestnuts on the streets of Bath," said one man. "They don't sell them any other time but Christmas. Snowy streets and roast chestnuts on the little pushcarts, that's Christmas."

"We was awful poor," said Alfred, "but I looked in the window of a big house once and saw the roast goose and a family all together with toys and a real music box. When I got back to the prison, my pa made me a rocking horse from a cushion and a piece of cradle. I'd rather a-had that," he added loyally, "than all them toys whut breaks so easy."

Christmas with Polly, Johnny thought. *What would it be like?* The two of them in a little cottage, with snow coming down like feathers and the bell ringers at the door and nuts to crack before the fire. And Polly in a dressing gown of pink—always pink for Polly—her fine hair loose around her shoulders, putting her hands up to his face, pulling his face close—

"Johnny!" Harvey's elbow dug him in the ribs. "Your turn."

"Huh? Oh—well, Christmas at boarding school was terrible. None of the boys was wanted home, and the masters ate all the goodies and—and we had boiled potatoes," Johnny finished lamely.

The men glared at him. "My, my," said Old Burgoo. "Our Johnny does add a pinch o' spice to the party, don't he?"

"Christmas is families," one of the men said, wiping his eyes.

"We're headed for home," Pearce said in a hurry, sensing homesickness. "Headed westward for Brazil to catch the winds, then north to Newfoundland, then easterly. Long about April we'll see England. Now let's show off our knot tying. How's young Alfred coming along?" He handed around short lengths of rope, and Alfred proudly demonstrated a running bowline.

"Marlinespike hitch!" Pearce called out, and Harvey slipped it over a belaying pin quick as a squint. The mate tossed him a coffee bean. Harvey popped it into his mouth and chewed.

"Cat's-paw!"

Johnny knotted his rope over his foot, almost like a double slip knot. "Coffee bean!" he cried, and the mate threw him one.

"French bowline!"

That was harder, and the older seamen finished up first.

"Double wall and double crown!"

Johnny unraveled his rope, then forgot how to do the knot. Rufus worked at his rope end until it looked like an enormous rose in bud. "Coffee bean, thank you kindly."

Harvey and the other old tars could do a diamond knot and bowline on a bight.

Old Burgoo ducked himself below deck and after a few minutes came back cuddling a little canvas bag in his crippled fingers. "Now, me hearties, I'll show ye a treasure of a knot, a thing not seen afore by mortal eye." He pulled a thin cord from the sack, and Johnny saw three knots tied in it.

"This here was gived to me by a witch woman on the Isle of Man," he chattered. "Oh, I paid dearly for it, ten shillings, I did."

"You *paid* good English coin for a cord with three knots in it?" asked Johnny.

"Listen a piece till I tell. Old Burgoo has been stuck in the Doldrums so many times, I asked the witch woman what's to be done. She called in the wind and tied it up in knots. 'Undo the first knot,' says she, 'and you'll get a nice wind. Undo the second, a storm. Undo the third knot, a fierce gale! You must take all three knots, or none,' says she. So Old Burgoo got hisself wind for when we're caught on this voyage without any."

Johnny reached out his hand to examine the cord, but Old Burgoo drew back. "Oh, no, ye don't, me lad. The captain will command when he wishes the wind. And the other two knots must never be undone. I'll be burning the cord after I use the first knot."

"Stuff and nonsense, then!" Johnny turned away, but from the corner of his eye, he saw the cook stow the little bag under his shirt.

Day after day, week after week, the ship held to a westerly course, trying to catch the homeward winds. Every day Johnny went aloft to shackle in the chain sheets that held the lower corners of the sail, and every night he loosed them. He taught young Alfred the rigging.

Johnny read all the books on the captain's shelf in his cabin, except one. *The Imitation of Christ* by Thomas a Kempis did not attract him. He knew the man was a German preacher who lived in the late thirteen hundreds, but religion was the last thing he wanted to read about.

Time wore on, and ship life was so routine that he finally took the book aloft with him in the crow's nest one day. "Better than playing mumblety-peg on my fingers," he sighed. "Oh, for a good storm!"

A storm in his soul began after reading a few chapters. The old conflict between right and wrong and how he had tried to be good many years ago, how he really *loved* goodness at one time, and his miserable failures, his bad life. For he quickly admitted to himself that he was bad. No one had to argue that he was a sinner. He *knew* he was a sinner, lost even beyond hope.

"Very quickly there will be an end of thee here; look what will become of thee in another world," he read.

"Bah! Another world! Tales to scare young'uns," he scoffed aloud. But deep in his heart there was a fear. *What if these things be true?*

"What answer shall you make to God who knoweth all your wickedness?" Johnny twisted around to see who spoke. No, the words he read in the book jumped off the page and came alive.

He read for an hour, growing more angry each moment. He *had* tried to be good years ago. Once he went three months without eating meat or talking to anyone, thinking it would help fix his mind on God. He used to punish himself, but he couldn't change.

"For He Himself is our sanctification and redemption." Kempis was quoting the Bible, he noted. He didn't care what the big words meant; they meant nothing to him. It couldn't be true, because it didn't work. He'd tried so hard. He had been sincere, those years he spent with his father. Why didn't God accept him?

He closed the book and looked out to sea. *What if these things be true?* The ship's bow swished through the water, rose and fell steadily, enough to rock a man asleep. The ship was a giant cradle for them all, but right underneath death waited.

What if these things be true? Johnny shook his head to clear the words away. Then he had an idea. If he destroyed the book, the thoughts would be gone.

On deck, below, some of the men were sleeping, and no one would see him. He aimed over the lee side, drew back his arm, and pitched the book into the ocean. The book spun up in a high arch, the gold edges sparkling in the sunshine, then fell swiftly, terribly, into the endless deeps of the sea.

"You have thrown away your soul!" For an instant he saw the dark stranger again, heard his fearful laughter, saw the flames kindled for him, and the ring sinking under the water, gone forever.

Only for an instant. "I will settle this once and for all time!" Johnny screamed to the sky, bashing his fist against the mast.

What if these things be true? The still, small voice persisted. Was it Steenie's voice? His mother's voice? No, only his own weakness. "Shut up," he commanded. "Shut up forever! Let me alone!"

A door closed in his mind. The pages of an open book flopped over, and the cover slammed tight. A small light flickering like a dying candle was snuffed out.

When a man came to relieve him, Johnny climbed down and headed for bed. No more thinking, no more reading religious books, no more trying for the impossible.

He woke up in darkness to hear loud voices. Raising up on an elbow, he strained his ears. An argument between the captain and Pearce. Dropping over the side of his hammock, he tiptoed to the cabin door.

"If we get a squall," Pearce said irritably, "I think we should hove to. I was mate on a ship where the captain didn't waste precious time in getting home. We kept the sea and wind three points forward of the beam. She rolled, but she didn't labor or pound. This ship is dry and cracked from the tropics. She won't stand much. We rode easily when we hove to, and a good man on the helm kept the rudder under control. We didn't broach or slew around."

"And I say that's too dangerous!" Captain Bigalow's voice was heavy with anger. "You are the *mate,* sir, not the captain! Take care that you not get logged as encouraging mutiny."

"Mutiny!" Pearce choked on his anger. "Captain, this is only a suggestion to you. I don't discuss our business with the crew."

"Take care you don't. I've been in many a gale, and I don't need advice from anyone!"

"When I captained a ship—."

"Aye, she foundered and went to the bottom!"

A door slammed, and Johnny tiptoed back to bed. So the ship was dry and cracked, was she? And no wonder, lying in the tropics so long just so the captain could stuff every available inch with cargo. Wasting precious time, was he? Aye, they hadn't caught a good wind yet.

Johnny dangled his legs over the edge of the hammock. He could hear Old Burgoo snoring like a goat. Very slowly he crept over until he was standing by the cook. Old Burgoo's shirt was open, and with the razor tip of his knife, Johnny lifted the string around the cook's neck and cut it and caught the key as it fell.

Old Burgoo's sea chest was crammed with junk from a dozen peddlers, but Johnny found the little bag. Opening the pouched end, he held the cord with its three knots. He dropped the bag inside the chest, locked it, and laid the key in Old Burgoo's open hand. The cook slept so soundly he could have sweet dreams in an earthquake.

Johnny knelt by the light of a candle stub and loosened the first knot. Such nonsense, believing in charms and witches and magic. But they needed a good wind to get home—and—who knows? What could be lost?

He untied the knot and climbed into his hammock and fell sound asleep. When the watch woke him, it was early morning, and he felt the ship racing before a wind. The crew were all talkative and happy. They had caught the trade winds and were homeward bound in a hurry.

Just happenstance, Johnny thought. Old Burgoo knew. After breakfast he hunted Johnny and said, "Old Burgoo is missin' somethin' that belongs to him, and him alone. Johnny, give it back, and I'll not say anything."

"Cheeky fellow you are," Johnny said rudely. "You have naught I'd covet."

"You young popinjay! You should be whipped at a cart's tail, you should. The devil's own offspring," Old Burgoo sputtered. "Poor Steenie would rise up in judgment on you."

"Shut up about Steenie!" Johnny said hotly. "Blinkin' rag-bag—."

" 'Tis you that's the thievin' spiv! You'll send us to the bottom yet!"

Johnny strode away and didn't speak to Old Burgoo after that. The wind blew freshly, and the ship sailed along, but not fast enough for Johnny. A good storm wouldn't hurt anyone and would strengthen the wind for them.

When he was alone, he took the cord from around his neck and picked out the second knot. Maybe a storm in the air could quiet the storm in his mind, like a pain in the foot took one's thoughts from a pain in the head.

Untied! *Storm, come upon us, break us on rocks, sink us, drive us down to hell! What do I care?*

Johnny ate his bean soup and hard knob of cheese and felt the air grow cooler. He strolled on deck and heard the mate yell, "Reduce sail!" Riggers climbed aloft as lightning penciled the sky and thunder rolled.

Johnny took out the cord and held it in his hand as the ship began to plunge, the wind whine and tease, and the sky blacked out.

"All hands!" roared Pearce, and Johnny had only a few seconds to work. His fingers picked the knot loose, worked it open, then out. Out. The cord was smooth, and he threw it overboard.

With a brutal slash of wind and water, the gale hit them like a broadside. Johnny clung to the bulwark, shook his fists at heaven, and screamed a duet with the gale, endless screams like a lost soul.

13

The Big Storm

The ship ran under half sail in the storm, caught by surprise. The captain ordered the helmsman to tack, bringing the ship's bow through the wind, beating to windward. The ship swung through twelve points of the compass, skidding sideways through the water. As the storm grew worse tacking was impossible, the winds were too strong.

"Throw her up into the wind! Back all square sails!" Captain Bigalow stood by the helmsman and shouted to Pearce.

Pearce shook his head. "Gale winds now!" he shouted back to the captain. "Put the rudder hard over! Boxhaul!"

"You fool! Go below, I say!" Captain Bigalow's face turned an angry purple. "I'll see you swing for this!" Johnny couldn't hear the mate's reply for the wind. He saw only his mouth, like a cat's lips, drawn back in silent protest.

Water sluiced through the scupper openings at the deck line. The helmsman roped himself fast, and the men laboring clamped knees and arms around anything that would hold them.

"John! Go below and fetch me a knife!" Captain Bigalow

153

grasped his arm and shouted in his ear. "Tell Rufus to batten
hatches and lash down the boats. Tell Harvey to rig the life-
lines across the deck. This gale took us all off our guard."

Hand over hand Johnny inched along the railing, then in a
lull ran across the deck and down the steps to the cabin. A
nameless sailor dashed past, and Johnny stopped him. "Take
this knife to the captain at the helm."

The sailor snatched the knife and went on deck. In the galley
saucepans hopped off the stove and splattered hot soup all over
the floor. Old Burgoo was trying to save the vegetables from
being washed away. He threw armfuls of potatoes into the
oven and slammed the door shut. The sea rushed through the
galley, soaking them, washing away everything loose.

"Tie the sacks to the leg of the stove!" the cook shrieked.
"Help me save 'em!"

"Captain wants me," Johnny yelled. "Tie 'em yourself!"

"This here storm was awful sudden-like," Old Burgoo said
between waves. "I was a-leanin' against the main mast and
lookin' up at the sails anglin' and thinkin' them right purty,
like lookin' straight up a lighthouse. All on a sudden the wind
touched the topsail and came down the chimney! Johnny, you
monkeyed with them knots. Our blood'll come on your head
for this."

"Rot! We needed a storm sooner or later. This is pushing us
home faster."

Bunks smashed, sea chests upended, pants, shirts, and
stockings welded together in a useless mass. The crew's quarters beneath the fo'c'sle flooded, water sloshed under the
swinging hammocks. They hadn't time to even take them
down. In the cabin, the officer's bedding was soaked.

A sailor shoved between them, stopped, and said, "Matey,
good thing you didn't take the knife up to the captain—Pat
was washed overboard just as he handed it over. He's gone. We
can't lower the boat in this gale."

Drowned in his place! Johnny stared at the cook. "Aye,

we're cursed," said Old Burgoo grimly. "You see? That's only the beginnin' o' sorrows."

"She's filling up fast," said the other man. "Upper timbers torn away—we're going to wreck!"

Johnny hurried up on deck to help. The captain hailed him. "John! John! Set the men to the pumps—we're going down!"

Sinking! Johnny saw Harvey and ran, holding to the lifeline, to give Harvey the order. "Man the pumps, all hands you can get! We're sinking!"

"Where's Pearce?"

"Mutiny! He gave orders to the helmsman against captain's word. Hanged if I know what's best to do now."

"Was there no warning for this?"

Johnny shook his head and looked away. "Hurry, now."

Old Burgoo floated by on a wall of water, a tin pail in each hand. "She's stove in on the starboard side, aft," he said. "Send some o' the lads to bail water."

"No hands left over," Johnny said. "Bail it yourself."

Old Burgoo gave him a reproachful look before a wash of water swept him away.

On deck, Johnny worked his way along the lifeline to the bow. Breakers higher than the masts roared toward them, but the ship rode up, down the other side, into a hellish, boiling gully. Men worked to stop the leaks with bedding, clothes, pieces of wood, anything they could find. Green seas crashed over the bow. There were still men aloft, trying to take in the sail with frozen, numb fingers along the ice-coated yards. The ship was near Newfoundland and the weather cold.

"Set the mainsail to keep her steady!" Captain Bigalow shouted at him. "John, I'm making you first mate, until this is over. Afterward, I'll have Pearce in irons."

"Yes, sir!" Johnny couldn't have been more surprised. Now they were walled in by water. Smeary clouds heavy with rain hung just above the masts. The rain, studded with icy shot, cut his face and lodged in his beard.

"Put four men at the helm!" the captain called. "We can't hold it alone."

Johnny fought his way through the crests of wave, which raked the deck, and found the men. A sail blew out, and three men tumbled into the sea. The ship half broached, then by a miracle righted itself. Johnny fell hard on one knee but held tight to the rope.

Now the sails were in ribbons. The yardarms lay splintered in their slings. The scream of sea and wind, grinding of rigging, ranged all up and down the notes of a hideous scale.

Johnny found the captain, who sent him below to help pump. Rufus was there with Alfred, who looked greenish and sick. "Cheers!" said Johnny to him. "This won't last long. We'll soon laugh at it over a glass of wine."

Alfred bent his head over his work, with no answer. Rufus motioned Johnny aside. "It's too late, now," he said. "We're going under!" Tears stood in his eyes.

Johnny worked at the pumps for six hours, then almost dead with cold and aching in every muscle, went on deck to find the captain. He was lashed at the helm, alone, his face gray and pulled tight with weariness and worry.

"John, take the helm. There's no other man to relieve me. If you're a praying man, which I have reason to doubt— well, if there's a ghost of a prayer in you—pray—for we are doomed!"

Gusty wind slopped the angry water along the deck; then a frightening silence fell over the ship.

"The real gale starts now," the captain said, passing his hand over his face. "Be prepared, John, you're an able seaman, and you're at the helm, for I shall drop dead if I don't go below to rest."

"By all means go, sir, I'll be all right. Nothing must happen to you, for all our sakes."

The wind started up again.

"She'd have sunk long ago," the captain said, "save for the

cargo, mainly wood and beeswax, very light it is and floats. But I fear the water has ruined it."

The ship plowed through heavy swells, rose up, rode high, plunged down a great wall of water. The sea again drenched them and made talk almost impossible.

"Can you hold her steady?"

"Aye, aye, sir."

"I'll put all hands to the pumps."

Men rolled like barrels across the deck, crashing into the bulwark, struggling to gain footing, rolling back again, a tangle of limbs and broken wreckage.

"Three pairs of broken legs!" Captain Bigalow yelled. "Hold to the course, John, for there's nothing else to do, and may God aid us."

"Aye, sir. If that doesn't work, then the Lord have mercy on us!"

The instant he said the words, he was struck with their meaning. He'd prayed! For the first time in his life, he had uttered a prayer! And he asked for mercy!

He roped himself to the helm, and as every wave broke over his head he expected it was the last for him. Now he was afraid to die, but he longed to get it over with and find out what his fate would be.

Wretched, famished with hunger, he had a gnawing rodent in his stomach. Drinking water was plentiful, but the awful strain of work began to tell on him.

Some of the men were so exhausted and seasick it took them three hours to furl a sail, a ten-minute job otherwise.

Out of the darkness and pitiless sea a face appeared. Rufus. "Old Burgoo washed overboard," he said. "A wave came hunting him, licked through the galley, and just up and took him. Men working around the clock at the pumps, for she's filling up fast. We're pumping out 120 tons of water an hour. Keep her steady, Johnny, and I'll bring you some vittles later."

He was gone, and Johnny didn't even have time to mourn Old Burgoo. He saw the foremast struck by lightning, flare up in fire an instant, then crack and drop into the sea as the ship rolled on her port side. Two men, burned and stunned, fell facedown on the deck and drowned in the swilling water.

The wheel fought and struggled in his hands as the tiller below was swung about by the powerful sea. The mast, yards, sails, and most of the rigging hung over the ship's side, beating against the ship, threatening to sink her. A few men worked trying to unrig the mess and set it loose.

Only the mainmast was still standing. As Johnny fought the wheel's thrust he saw the mainmast spring a crack that raced up one side. *Timber dry inside,* he thought. The mast cracked and fell over the lee side of the ship, missing the deck by a pinch.

The whole world reeled. Day and night were alike. For twelve hours Johnny stayed at the helm, his body salted down in the lash of waves. Sleet like needles pained his face, then numbed it.

A two-ton yardarm crashed down on deck, leveling the foredeck. The ship strained up, then plunged down into deep, watery pits, forced up again by the violent sea—up—down—up—down. His hands lost all feeling, and he willed them to hang on. The wind's teeth tattered his shirt, and he shivered without pause.

Now the monster waves measured a mile from peak to peak. The ship rode high on the crests, then dashed into valleys of black water.

Every time Johnny looked over his shoulder, he saw an immense body of water, higher than a house. In front of him yawned a deep pit. The ship roared down into the ghastly pit and swiftly rode up its side to the top before the mountain of water in back could overtake it. Every four seconds this up-and-down journey was repeated. All this time the boiling, foaming sea was only five yards below the deck.

Twelve long hours and Johnny had time to think. He remembered his dream, the warnings, the times his life was spared, the many times he'd mocked God and His Holy Word.

He came to the conclusion there never was such a sinner as himself, completely bad through and through. His sins were too great to be forgiven, even supposing the Bible was true.

Snatches of Scripture he'd read long ago came to mind: "I have called and ye refused." Too late now. "Forsaken the right way and gone astray." That was himself all right. No hope.

He thought of Jesus, who died for sins not His own. He knew the story, but he'd never believed it. "Would it was true," he said, but the wind blew the words back in his mouth.

Men call God "Father," he thought. *How dare they do that?* If only *he* could. His cry was more like that of a sea gull, just crying to be heard or to be saved from danger.

If there is an Almighty God, then I need an Almighty Saviour to come between my soul and God, for my sin is ever before me, he thought. *But I've mocked and cursed Him. He would never have anything to do with me.*

March twenty-first, the day he would never forget, finally ended and another man came to take a trick at the wheel. The wind gradually died down, and the storm was over. All the livestock—pigs, sheep, and chickens—had been washed overboard. Only one week's food supply was left. Most of the sails were blown away.

After Johnny rested up, Captain Bigalow called him into his cabin. "I thank you for your loyalty," he said, "and for your seamanship put to the test in the storm. I'm entering an account of it in the log. Pearce will be demoted. Since he led none of the men astray, there will be no further punishment, but I'll not ship with him again. The wind is fair, now, and we are about one hundred leagues from land. I should judge we are off the coast of northern Ireland. We'll go on short rations, but there is plenty of drinking water—six large butts still untapped."

"Old Burgoo . . . ," Johnny began sadly. "Maybe you would read prayers."

"Ho, the blighter is sound asleep in his bed. He did get washed overboard, but fortunately he'd tied a rope to his ankle, and somebody hauled him back up, none the worse for a ducking. He'll live to scrape the pots again."

Four or five days passed, and the crew cleaned up the wreckage the best they could. Johnny was awakened one morning by the joyful shout, "Land, ho!" from the watch. He joined the others in climbing up on deck to see.

The day was dawning, and only twenty miles away a mountainous coast rose out of the sea, with a few little islands at the tip.

"Ireland! Ireland!" they all shouted, clasping hands and smacking backs. "By tomorrow we'll be ashore, then home!"

"Use up the last of the brandy in water," Captain Bigalow commanded. "Finish up the bread, for we won't be needing it, and it's moldy."

"I certainly *hope* it proves to be land," said Pearce sullenly.

The men would have set upon him with their fists, except for the captain's presence. They began to argue and debate over what part of Ireland it could be.

Johnny went aloft and with his spyglass watched the land. The thought of soon seeing Polly excited him, and he didn't read or smoke. Then it occurred to him how very strange that was—not to want to smoke! Nor to swear and curse! He was different, a changed person, ever since he had cried to God for mercy. He still didn't understand what happened to him.

A cry of rage and disappointment went up from below, and he looked again at the land. Turning a blushing rose from the sun, the island slowly faded away. A mirage! There was nothing there at all!

The fair wind changed to a sharp wind from the southwest, and the ship was blown off course again. Captain Bigalow paced the deck, snuffing to see which way the wind blew. His memory was short; he forgot all the help Johnny was during the storm and remembered only his badness. Day after day he blamed him for all their trouble.

"I took a Jonah on board when I took you," he sneered. "If I were to throw you overboard, now, we'd be at peace."

The food was gone and the ship so wrecked that it barely floated. The wind blew them afar north, out of the shipping lanes, so there was no hope of rescue. The men lived on half a salted codfish each day, and even Old Burgoo shriveled up into himself as he cut up the fish, refusing to talk.

The captain's temper was worn thin as the weather turned bitterly cold and everyone owned only the rags he wore on his back. "A pox on you," he told Johnny. "You jinxed every ship you ever sailed on. 'Twill be a miracle that I don't throw you over the side."

Johnny silently agreed, but noted the change in himself. He didn't lose his temper or plot revenge anymore. Most astonishing of all, the cursing that was a part of his being was no longer heard. He wasn't even tempted.

The crew lived in fear of starvation or of being obliged to eat the ones who died, and still they didn't sight land. Johnny was beginning to think the Bible might be true after all; he felt such a sense of relief from fear. He kept praying that God would rescue them, and one day the wind turned in such a way that the ship could safely head for land and still keep the broken part out of the water. No human being could have arranged that. All hands worked together cheerfully and patched hammocks and bed covers to sling up as sails.

Slowly the ship bore to the east until on April eighth land was seen. The next day she anchored in Lough Swilly, Ireland, four weeks after the big storm, just as the last vittles were boiling in the pot. The ship had been reported as missing for eighteen months.

Within two hours another gale began to blow, and if the ship had not reached land, she would have foundered. Then the captain discovered the five remaining water kegs were empty, not full, as he assumed. There was no drinking water left at all, not even to keep them one more day at sea.

When Johnny heard those things, he thought: *There is a God who hears and answers prayer!*

14

Amazing Grace

Lough Swilly was a deep, narrow tongue of the Atlantic Ocean cutting into the land at the northern tip of Ireland, a safe harbor for ships. Only ten miles away was the town of Londonderry, with boardinghouses and churches. Directly east lay the borders of Scotland and England.

The rest of the crew stayed behind to repair the ship, but Johnny determined to reach his father and Polly. He borrowed money from Captain Bigalow and started out the next morning.

"We'll meet again," he said to Old Burgoo. "When I'm captain of a ship, you'll be cook. I promise you."

Strips of filmy fog lifted and vanished as he walked the road to Londonderry, dressed only in the sailor clothes he wore aboard ship. The spring air was cold, and he hurried to keep warm, beating his arms against his sides.

The lonely, wild, harsh mountain country turned to endless acres of greenery as he drew near the town. Piles of bare rocks lay fallen along the twisty road. He passed small lakes set in

163

the green like blue jewels. More rocky fields, caves, peat bogs.
"Ho, there! Can you give me some drink?"

He met an old horse pulling a milk wagon driven by a
skinny man with a stocking cap on his head. Johnny made him
understand, by signs, that he was a sailor on his way home.
The man smiled and gave him a dipper full of milk, still warm.

"My thanks," Johnny said. In the old days he would have
knocked the farmer out of the wagon and swiped the horse.

Here and there he saw a cottage with its roof thatched with
rushes from the bog. The outside walls sparkled white in the
sun from the limewash spread over them.

At the Seafarer's Inn, in Londonderry, Johnny found that
the owners, Alden Dulaine and his wife, spoke good English.
They gave him a room with a huge stone fireplace, where a turf
fire warmed the hearth.

Around an oak table in the dining room, Johnny feasted on
potato-onion soup, cottage cheese, and round loaves of bread
marked with a cross and baked in a black kettle over the fire.
Dark wooden beams formed the ceiling and made the room
dim and cozy.

"Have you church services here?" he asked Alden. There
was a hunger in him to understand his past life, the escapes
from death, the answer to prayer after the storm.

"Prayers twice a day," Alden said. "The vicar reads prayers
and answers questions. Sundays there's a rousing good sermon."

Johnny sat in Reverend Hempstead's living room, feeling as
out of place as a ship on dry land. Though he wore gentleman's
clothes, borrowed from Alden, he knew he was nothing but a
sailor.

Reverend Hempstead, the vicar, was middle-aged and
cheerful, with laughing eyes. He put Johnny at ease by saying,
"Lad, I shipped out on two voyages around the Horn before I
got my education. In those days, life at sea was *rough!*"

"I doubt it's changed, sir," said Johnny, smiling back at him.
Then he remembered why he was there. Ashamed and fearful,

he told of his past life, his sin, troublemaking, dirty tricks, all of it.

He ended by saying, "So, vicar, God was following me all the time, but I was running. I didn't even believe in Him, but when I cried, He answered. Our safe return in a broken ship with a scrap of sail and no food or water left was a miracle. Now what must I *do* to be accepted by God? What must I *do* to have sins forgiven? What must I *do* before I can come before God in prayer?"

"Lad, it's been *done!*"

"W-what?"

"The Lord Jesus Christ has *done* everything for you. All you need do is believe it and take the gift of salvation and eternal life."

Johnny sat on the edge of the chair and stared at the vicar with questioning eyes. "Sir—I don't understand. I must suffer and be punished. I must *do* something to gain God's favor. How can God accept an ungodly one as I am?"

"He not only will receive you as His son; He will make you holy!"

Johnny sank back in his chair, astounded. Surely this man of God would not jest with him or lead him astray. Ah, he had it! He would ask him to prove it. If it was in Holy Scripture, then it must be true. For he believed the Bible. The few times he had looked into the Book, a strange feeling seized his heart as though a Spirit made the words come alive. Once he read in the Bible that there *was* a Holy Spirit who taught people the truth.

"Vicar," he said, "is that in the Bible? You understand, it's so new to me, so strange, so hard to believe—."

"I do understand." Reverend Hempstead reached behind him and took down a heavy family Bible from the shelf. "There is one little word you need to understand, and that will unlock all the mystery of salvation."

"A little word?"

"Yes—*grace.*"

"Grace? What does it mean?"

"What do *you* think it means?"

Johnny thought hard. Such a little word and how to explain it? "Grace—well—it's like—well, the king is gracious, he shows grace—he grants us things we don't deserve—."

"That's it!" the vicar said in excitement. "You figured it out for yourself. You don't *deserve* anything from God."

Johnny's face fell. "Aye, that I know. Haven't I been saying it? I must reform and wait awhile before I come to God. I'm not ready. I will try harder to live a good life. Already the habit of cursing is gone." He broke off to think. "Why, it was taken away from me!" he said, startled. "I never could have broken that foul habit! Faith, and I believe my tongue belonged to Satan. But the habit was *taken away!*"

Reverend Hempstead nodded, rocking back and forth. "Again, you are seeing it for yourself. God worked in your life. Johnny, you *can't* change yourself. No man can. Oh, maybe on the outside, to fool others, but the heart remains sinful. God is holy, and no one could come near to Him with a sinful heart."

"No one has to tell me that!" Johnny cried, close to tears. "Day and night, every waking minute, my sin is before me, like a mountain on my back! I see no hope for me, no way at all, for I truly tried to be better, years ago, and I failed."

"Let's see what God's Word says." The vicar opened the Bible to the book of Romans, chapter four, verse five: " 'But to him that worketh not, but believeth on him that justifieth the ungodly, his faith is counted for righteousness.' "

"God justifies the ungodly? That's me. What's *justify* mean?"

"Made good, right, holy, right with God."

"My faith makes me good in God's sight?"

"Exactly. Now here's another verse, same book, chapter five, verse twenty: '. . . Where sin abounded, grace did much more abound.' Put it into your own words, Johnny."

"Where there was great sin—like in my life—there was great grace, great favors that I don't deserve." Johnny thought it over in silence. *Could such a wonderful thing be true? God for-*

*gives those who deserve to be punished? God favors those who
deserve no favors? Gives them eternal life just for believing?*

"But I'm such a *black* sinner," he said in despair. "I'm a
criminal, for I broke the law over and over. I just don't feel I
can come to God. I can't—I can't! My sin deserves *death,* death
forever; how can I come to God? What must I *do* first?"

"Now we're back to where we began," said the vicar. "The
Lord Jesus Christ, God in the flesh, has *done* it all. He paid
with His life's blood. You need not come to God alone—you
come in Jesus' Name, and in Him, God will receive you and
pardon you.

" 'For when we were yet without strength, in due time Christ
died for the ungodly,' " read the vicar. "Romans again, chapter
five, verse six."

"Who wrote that part of the Bible?" Johnny demanded.

"An ex-murderer, the chief of sinners, an ungodly man who
was saved by grace."

"Aw, 'tain't true." Johnny was so shocked he lapsed into
sailor talk. "Begging your pardon, sir, I didn't mean that.
Wasn't he a saintly sort of fellow?"

"He was saved by grace when he was Saul of Tarsus, a sinner. Afterward, God gave him some of His own righteousness,
and then, yes, I suppose you could call him saintly. *Afterward."*

"Suppose I try to believe, but don't have enough faith?
That's just how I feel now. I want to believe, but. . . ."

Reverend Hempstead turned the Bible pages. " 'For by
grace are ye saved through faith; and that not of yourselves: it
is the gift of God: Not of works, lest any man should boast.'
Ephesians, chapter two, verses eight and nine. God will pro-
vide even the faith, Johnny. He even gives repentance to a
man, if he asks."

"I'm sorry enough about my sin, all right," Johnny said.
"But I feel that perhaps I haven't been sorry *enough.* I should
spend a week weeping over my sin and praying. Such a thing
as salvation can't be settled in a minute."

"Yes, it can. Remember that unbelief is the worst sin of all.

While you hold out and hold back, that is unbelief. You are calling God a liar. The main point is this: Do you feel you need a Saviour, or can you save yourself?"

"Oh, I *need* a Saviour!" Johnny said earnestly. "I *need* a go-between. But I'm the *worst* sinner! Can God save the *worst?*"

"You're wrong. Saul of Tarsus was the worst. Then I am next." Reverend Hempstead offered his Bible. "Take this and read more, Johnny. Keep it as long as you like."

Johnny stood up, holding the Bible. "I'm not ready, sir, I hope you forgive me. I can't believe it's for me."

"Your unbelief is worse than anything you have ever done," said the vicar sadly. "Johnny, I'll be praying for you until I hear you have peace with God. Don't ever forget—it is all of grace."

Alone in his room, Johnny read from the Bible for hours. He read until Alden rapped on the door and invited him to go hunting.

"A nice bird in the pot would taste good on a chilly eve," he said. "The mayor himself is going with us."

Johnny closed the Book and pulled on a warm jacket the landlord offered him. They walked down the lane, past thatched cottages, and he heard the loud thump-thump of the handlooms as the busy housewives wove tweed cloth, in all colors of the rainbow, from their own sheep's wool. The finished warm tweeds would be taken to market in donkey carts and sold in England.

As they walked beyond the town and into the woods red-cheeked youngsters played with dolls in wagons.

"If we climb atop this bank," said Alden, "we will be able to see nests and a plain where the birds feed."

Johnny carried his loaded gun under his arm and pulled himself up the steep bank with one hand, catching fast to roots sticking out of the dirt. Halfway up, his foot slid in the loose stones, and he nearly rolled down the hill.

"Ho, there! Lend a hand . . . !" Suddenly there was a blast of fire near his right ear, pain, and blood drops falling down his shirt. His hat fell to the ground, shot to pieces.

"John, are you all right?" The mayor, a stout, red-haired man, reached a long arm to him. "Are you hurt? What happened?"

Johnny pulled himself to the top and lay on his face for a minute. "My gun fired," he said. "Guess I wasn't too careful. I felt it go by my ear."

Alden knelt beside him and held his handkerchief to the cut. His hand shook. "Near blew your head off," he said. "A fraction closer and you'd be a dead man."

Johnny handed his gun over. "I'm out of practice," he said, "and my hands are shaky. Do you mind if I go back?"

The men patted him on the arm and told him to nap before dinner; they'd bring the bird for the pot.

Johnny almost ran back to the inn. He didn't care what the village people thought as they saw him fly along. If he had died, he'd have gone to hell, for he'd heard the way of salvation and put it off. God spared his life again, but this time might be the last warning.

In his room he bolted the door and dropped on his knees by the bed. "Oh, God!" he cried. "I'm ready! Have mercy on me, save my soul for Jesus' sake, who died for me. I thank You for all the warnings, all the times You spared my life, Your *grace* to me." Now he understood all the meanings of that small word, for he had just experienced grace in the shooting accident.

"Lord Jesus, Saviour, I want to be Yours and Yours alone, forever." He saw that believing and coming to Jesus were one and the same. As he thought of the cross at Calvary and what it cost for his salvation, he marveled that he hadn't come sooner.

A river of joy welled up in his heart. He wasn't the old Johnny Newton—selfish, sneaky, hateful, nasty, cruel, dirty-minded—he was somebody new, made all over again. Clean. Forgiven. In Christ.

The Dulaines saw the change, for he couldn't hide it. To add to his happiness, a letter from his father came in the post.

"Son, I gave you up for dead, since nothing was heard from your ship for eighteen months. I have visited the Catletts at Kent and have given my permission and blessing for your marriage to Miss Polly. All you have to do is obtain her consent. If you come down to Liverpool, you will find me at the old lodgings. I am appointed governor of York Fort in Hudson's Bay and will sail from London shortly. You will improve your fortune if you go with me for three years. Your affectionate Father."

Affectionate Father. Oh, Father, I never really knew you. How I've disappointed you. Oh, the trouble and worry and grief I caused you, and still you care. We will meet again, and I will kneel and say, "Father, I have sinned against heaven and in your sight and am no more worthy to be called your son." I want to tell you what happened to me, for it is so hard to write it all.

Johnny answered the letter, explaining the change in him, saying he would try to get to Liverpool as soon as he could. The next letter was to Polly, telling her of his safe arrival, asking to see her. Did she wait—those eighteen months she thought him dead? Would she understand the change in him?

That Sunday, Johnny attended the village church to receive holy communion for the first time. Reverend Hempstead called it the Lord's Supper. Bread and grape juice was offered each one. "In remembrance of Me." Could he ever forget? *Not to my dying day,* Johnny thought. *Me, a wicked sinner, an enemy of God, lifted by His grace, loved by Him, bought with the price of blood, made* holy.

He closed his eyes to eat and drink. Broken body and shed blood. He found the Almighty Saviour he needed—a Saviour who could also keep him from sin and lead his steps and plan his life.

He left the church and notified the Dulaines that he must leave for Liverpool the next day. Catching a mail coach from town, he suffered through the long, bumpy ride to Belfast, then took passage on a ship for Liverpool.

He found his father's lodgings rented to a stranger and his father gone. The landlady said he had left earlier than he planned for Fort York.

Johnny walked to Mr. Manesty's office, down by the docks, where early-morning fog blanketed the town, blunted the outline of houses and stores, and made morning seem like twilight.

Next to a chandler's shop, Johnny found Mr. Manesty in his office, posting a list of ships' sailing dates.

"Johnny Newton!" Mr. Manesty threw his arms around him and welcomed him like a long-lost son. He was an elderly man with knobby, red cheeks and wisps of beard. "Johnny, we gave up the ship for lost! What perils on the sea you must have gone through!"

"Aye, and strange happenings, too." Johnny hardly knew how to begin or how to say it. "Mr. Manesty, sir, I'm not the same lad. I—I've got religion. No, I mean to say I have a Saviour, Christ the Lord." Feeling as though he were describing the Christmas story, he told Mr. Manesty of his conversion.

"Has my father indeed sailed to Fort York?" he then asked.

"Only yesterday. And what a pity you missed him by one day. Lad, I have been reading the log of Captain Bigalow and his account of Pearce and the trouble and how you stood by him and stuck at the helm through the worst storm of his career. Johnny, I've a ship ready to sail, and you're the captain for it. You have more than enough head knowledge, besides experience. What do you say?"

"Sir, it's what I've dreamed of. But my better judgment tells me to ship out as first mate on a voyage, before I attempt to command. As you must know, I was never very obedient or useful in the past. I want to learn to take orders before I give them."

Mr. Manesty looked disappointed. "Whatever you say, lad.

If you've had a change of heart, like you say, I'd trust you with any ship. There's nothing like faith in God to make a man dependable."

"I know God has forgiven me," Johnny said. "It's quite another thing to forgive myself. I've led others astray. I've done so much harm."

"The past is past. 'The blood of Jesus Christ, God's Son, cleans us from all sin.' Now, sir, I have a ship sailing in two weeks from Liverpool, a two-year voyage. Do you want to sign on as first mate?"

"Aye, aye, sir!"

"Johnny, I have an idea you'll want to spend the next two weeks visiting a certain young lady at Maidstone, Kent."

Johnny grinned. "If I may, sir. I'll be back on time, I promise. Now I have a favor to ask. Have you signed on a cook yet?"

"No, as a matter of fact I was wondering—."

"Old Burgoo. You know him? I never heard his real name."

"Who doesn't know Old Burgoo? You would like him for cook?"

"If he can be reached. He's on the *Newcomer,* at Lough Swilly."

"I'll arrange it." Mr. Manesty reached out and shook his hand warmly.

Johnny left the office and walked into the fresh spring air with all fog melted away. Wouldn't Old Burgoo's eyes pop when he saw him as first mate and knew the next voyage after that he'd command a ship!

15

The Cup of Love

May, 1748. The English countryside in Kent was green and flowered. The rolling hills stretched off as far as the eye could see as Johnny hiked along the road to Maidstone. Wild geese nested in the meadow, gabbling and chattering and annoying the larks, who flew into the air in a frenzy. As he drew near the Catletts' he could see a swan family gliding on the lake in back of the house.

Next door, a potter had moved his wheel and bench outdoors and was working with clay. Johnny's heart beat faster, until he thought he'd suffocate. Would she be there? Would she know him? Six years had passed. He was twenty-three years old. She was twenty.

He lifted his hand to knock, but before he could touch the door, it flew open and Mrs. Catlett, more plump and smiling than ever, threw her arms around him and hugged him close.

"Johnny Newton! We thought you drowned at sea! Come in, come in, the girls are here!"

Johnny looked past her and thought he was seeing a ghost! Polly, still fourteen, a beautiful child—no, of course not, it was

173

Catherine. He looked beyond her and saw Polly, the woman. A little taller, her long, gold hair pulled back at the neck and tied into a net, her eyes bigger and more blue and so serious. She was wearing dark brown, which only made her hair shine like fire and set off her dark eyelashes and soft, velvety brows. Her beauty lit up the dark hallway.

He took her hand and because the speech he planned on the way flew out of his mind, he bent and kissed it.

"John," she said simply. "How long it has been." Her voice was still soft and whispery.

"Polly. Did you get all my letters?"

"Yes, indeedy." Mrs. Catlett answered for her. "Come, sit down to dinner, Johnny. There's steak-and-kidney pie, ham, fresh eggs, some of Polly's bread, and Catherine's gooseberry jam."

Johnny ate heartily, enjoying each bite of home-cooked food, but his eyes followed Polly's every move. She poured the tea. Her little hands were pink with small, shell fingernails, clean and shiny. She lifted her fork with a bit of meat pie—her mouth was full and rosy, with crumbs at one corner. Adorable. Her face had lost its chubbiness and was a perfect oval, with the white skin of an English country girl.

"Six years! Why, I can't believe it!" Mrs. Catlett helped herself to more meat pie than was necessary for one so well fed. "Your father paid us such a nice visit, Johnny, and he looked so well and happy that you didn't drown."

Johnny felt his face flush, remembering the purpose of his father's visit. Polly was paying great attention to the way she spread the jam across her bread. She pricked it with the fork and made designs all around the edge before she looked up.

"What have you been doing these six years?" he asked awkwardly. There was still a stubborn set to her chin and a new poise in her manner.

"Catherine and I play chamber music with a small group that meets here," she replied.

"Flute, both of us," Catherine put in helpfully.

Mrs. Catlett filled the milk pitcher again. She pressed her lips together and eyed her daughter. "You'd best tell him," she said.

Johnny glanced at Polly, and the pulse in his neck began to skip beats, from holding his breath. Not wedded! Or promised? *Oh, God,* he prayed silently. *Don't let it be that.*

Polly looked at him steadily, though her cheeks turned pinkish. "I have been to the city on shopping trips, and I have seen how the poor live, how they have no church, for the big churches don't want them. They haven't the clothes to dress up for Sundays. . . ." She took a deep breath. "And I have seen the children growing up in the streets, with no knowledge of God. They turn to crime, for there is nowhere else to turn."

Johnny breathed easier. What was she trying to say?

"And I have decided to help them. And so I have!"

Johnny looked at Mrs. Catlett, puzzled. He didn't understand.

"Don't think it was my doing," Mrs. Catlett said smartly. "I don't think too much of her schemes, but her father *would* give in to her and help her with a little money, though he said Catherine was not old enough to go along."

Johnny looked from one to the other. What were they talking about?

"Just once a week," Polly said calmly. "John, if you saw how those poor folk live, you would no doubt help also."

"Help the poor?" Johnny said clumsily. "I don't understand. Do you send them money?"

"No, I send myself," Polly said firmly. "Since the church does not want the poor, I will take church to them."

"Why, you can't do that!" Johnny was horrified. "You don't mean you go a-visiting amongst the poor, down those streets of crime, among fallen women and drunken men!" He laid down his fork and stared at her.

"Don't think I began all this," Mrs. Catlett begged, tossing her head and plunking down a platter of ham. "Polly is not yet of age, but her father *does* indulge her and even encourages it."

Johnny forgot his shyness with the girl and said earnestly, "Polly, dear, you *mustn't* go to such places! The things that could happen to you, dear!"

"Mustn't?" The stubborn little chin lifted up, and her eyes flashed blue sparks.

"I—I mean—I mean that I wouldn't have an hour's peace in my mind if I thought you—I mean, what a worry to your mother this must be—I only mean to say—" He ended helplessly, looked down at his plate and thought how little he knew this girl.

"I don't go alone," Polly continued, sipping tea and nibbling her buttered bread. "Mama goes, though she protests all the way. Five other young women from our church and four men all go on a Friday night, and we sing hymns and read prayers, and a regular ordained minister from the Church speaks to the people who crowd in."

"In where?" asked Johnny, more confused than ever.

"Why, in the hall we've rented in Perry Lane in Drewbury. It's perfectly safe, John, and they are lovely people."

"Lovely! Perry Lane! Not in *Drewbury!*" Johnny was beginning to feel life at sea was not more surprising than this girl. "Do you mean that you are some sort of—missionary—to the lower class?"

"You simply would not believe what this girl has been into while you were gone, Johnny." Mrs. Catlett threw up her hands for heaven to witness. "It began with one shopping trip; then she saw a poor beggar woman not much older than herself, then the streetwalkers; then she poked about behind the shops and saw the broken-down houses by the ditch; then she gave three pence to a beggar and asked him questions; then she visited the awful cellars, crawling with lice and what-not; then she took a blanket to a family with four naked babies; and on and on she goes, and I do wish . . . ," Mrs. Catlett made motions with her hands behind Polly's back, ". . . and I do wish she'd settle down and. . . ." She left the word *marry* unsaid and filled Johnny's plate with more eggs.

"Mother, please don't make me sound like an idiot." Polly looked at Johnny gravely. "I did not know such awful things were in God's world until I went to the city. Who will help those people if we don't?"

"The church," Johnny said. "There's the churches open on Sundays."

"They don't want the poor," Polly explained. "Some of those people told me how they were turned away at the door for lack of fine clothes and water to bathe in."

Johnny drank tea silently. While he was at sea, thinking her safe at home, she'd been taking all kinds of risks, going places where the law was afraid to go, putting herself in danger.

"Polly is awfully brave," Catherine volunteered. "She makes the folks at church very angry, sometimes, 'cause she tells them *they* should be going out to look for people."

"The poor are poor because they drink up their wages and live wicked lives," Johnny said. " 'Tis their own fault. Why bother with them?"

"That's not true," retorted Polly. "They are bad because they never heard the Gospel preached to them. If they could get God's saving power, they could live holy lives, yes, even in slums. It occurred to me, only two years ago, how selfish I was."

Selfish? Darling Polly, selfish?

She saw the disbelief in his eyes and explained. "Yes, selfish. I have a Bible and a pastor and a church, and they have— nothing. Yet our Lord said the Gospel should be preached to the poor. The churches cater to the rich. They have shut out the poor."

Mrs. Catlett began clearing the table. "Johnny, this girl is a handful, but she's started something that other good Christians are watching. I do admit that two hundred souls on a Friday night is a nice beginning for a missionary work."

"Two hundred people!" Johnny shook his head from side to side in amazement. "Two hundred people come to your— church?"

"Yes, and we play our flutes and sing," Catherine said.

"You young folk go into the sitting room and talk while I do up the dishes," Mrs. Catlett ordered. "Johnny has only two weeks with us, and the time will fly."

The girls disappeared, and Johnny held back and said to Mrs. Catlett, "May I have your permission to speak to Polly, to ask her—."

"Only to wait two years," Mrs. Catlett said. "You are not ready to ask the other question yet, Johnny."

"Please—let me get a promise from her to wed. Please, dear Mrs. Catlett. So much could happen in two years."

Mrs. Catlett wiped her hands on her apron and stacked the greasy dishes. "Johnny, no. Let me give you one bit of Scripture from the Holy Book. Your father told me of the great change in you, and if it's real, you'll listen to me and not take your own way."

"Yes, ma'am," Johnny waited meekly.

"All right, then. From First Corinthians, chapter thirteen. Just two words, son, but let them guide you for the next two years. 'Love suffers.' "

"Love suffers," Johnny repeated wonderingly.

" 'Love suffers.' If you love our Polly, you will wait two more years until you can offer her a home and something secure. Love is willing to suffer for the one loved."

Johnny sighed deeply and went to find Polly. Catherine stopped him in the hall and pulled down his head to whisper in his ear. "Johnny, she's been busy quilting, too. She's made a dozen quilts, besides curtains and doilies, all ready for you-know-what!"

Johnny felt his face and ears grow warm. "Go along, Miss Spy. Don't trouble us now, and I'll give you a shilling tomorrow."

Catherine skipped with glee, made sure the sitting-room door shut behind Johnny, and tiptoed up the broad steps to her room.

Johnny crossed the room to where Polly stood by the window, opening the drapes. "I think your work among the poor is fine," he said. "It was just that I was surprised."

"Oh, John, if you could see the great needs. . . . But of course you've seen them—you've lodged in some of England's cities."

"Yes, I've seen the needs. But they're lower-class, Polly. One of their own should help them."

"Lower-class!" Polly faced him angrily. "And I say the day is coming when Christian people will see that we are one in Christ. The Bible does not teach class."

"Polly! Polly! You must have been reading books to make you like this!"

"Yes—the Bible."

He touched her arm lightly. "Polly, I shouldn't wonder that you've been changed through a Book, for something happened to me, too." And as they sat together on the sofa, he told her.

"Words have been running through my mind," he said after he finished. "Rhyming words. Oh, not real poetry, but just things I want to say about God's grace. If I wrote the words down—could you find a tune with your flute?"

"Perhaps." Polly laughed. "I never tried to write music."

"Then help me finish this rhyme. I started out: 'Amazing grace—how sweet the sound—.' Now I want a second line: 'That saved a—*something*—like me!' "

"*Sinner?*" Polly suggested.

"No, a word of one syllable. A short, snappy word that describes all I've been."

"*Bad person? Evildoer?*"

"No, no. Ah, I have it—a *wretch!*"

"John, that's too harsh," Polly protested.

" 'Saved a wretch like me. I once was lost. . . .' "

" '. . . but now am found,' " said Polly.

" 'Was blind—.' "

" 'But now I see.' "

"Polly, do you understand what *grace* means?"

"Let me think." She rubbed her forehead a minute, with her eyes closed. "Grace is all God wants to give me—a peaceful mind, joy in sorrow, love for others who may dislike me, patience when I've run out of patience, more faith, goodness. And I don't deserve any of it."

Johnny marveled at the little sermon. While God had been dealing with him, He had also taught this girl the same things. "And the Lord Jesus Christ made this possible," he added. "You know, grace even taught my heart to fear, but then grace relieved all my fears. I'll never forget the hour when I first believed, when I just cast myself on God's mercy."

"If we lived ten thousand years we could never thank Him enough," Polly added.

"Polly," said Johnny, for he was curious. "How could you even feel you are a sinner in need of grace, when you have lived a sheltered life at home; you have not been tempted in the ways I have; you have not committed crimes; you have not gone astray."

"Oh, but sin has burdened me—such pride, such selfishness, such discontent, such lack of prayer."

We have come in different ways, thought Johnny, *but we have both come to Christ. I have come through many dangers, toils, snares, but the same grace won us and is taking us both safely to heaven.*

"I'll write down all my thoughts on grace," he said aloud, "and you shall make a song of it. I have other rhymes milling about in my head. I'll have time to think when I'm at sea."

Polly half smiled and toyed with the pillow tassel as she looked at him. "John, I can see you as a minister in a church, preaching great sermons—on grace—while all sorts of people are welcomed in."

"Oh, no, I'm a seaman. Why, what delightful fancy you have, Polly, to imagine such a thing."

"No, it isn't my fancy. Your mother gave you to God for the ministry, when you were born. Mama told me so."

"Aye, but that was long ago." Johnny laughed at the notion of himself, in a frock coat and white collar, behind a pulpit, preaching to a church full of people. Why, he would faint away with embarrassment or forget the sermon or just turn and run away! He, the rough-tongued sailor—a preacher!

"Polly, I was offered command of a ship."

It was her turn to be startled. "Captain a ship? Oh, John, such an honor! Captain!" Her eyes shone.

"Yes, Captain Newton, Miss. Does this please you?"

"Oh, yes!" She clapped her hands with delight, and his heart leaped. "For as captain, John, you can read prayers and hold services and require everyone to attend. You could probably preach a little. No one would report the captain for making bold to preach."

"I see." Johnny's hopes came crashing down. "I thought maybe you were glad because it meant that after the voyage I could ask. . . ." He remembered his promise to Mrs. Catlett and fell silent.

Polly seemed not to understand. "John, as captain you would be over perhaps two hundred people; seamen who would listen to you and admire you. Seamen who were never welcome in the churches. You could take Bibles aboard and encourage the men to read for themselves—teach them to read if you had to—and wherever you put ashore, everyone would know that here is a ship's captain who is a Christian. . . ."

Little missionary! Johnny decided to settle all he was allowed to settle—now.

"Polly, that isn't exactly what I meant. Besides, I've refused to captain the ship. I'm shipping out as first mate so I will learn to take orders—something I should have learned years ago. When I come back in two years, I will have a very important question to ask you. I can't ask it now. I can only ask this. . . ." He took her hand, and she didn't pull away. Her hand was soft and so tiny, with frilly lace falling over her wrist. "Polly, will you wait two more years? Until I can ask that other question?"

Her golden head drooped over the hand, and she was suddenly quiet.

"Polly?"

No answer.

He slipped his arm around her waist, ever so gently, and moved a little closer. "Polly, dear, will you wait two years? For I love you with all my heart."

Her hairnet had worked itself loose, and the golden hair spilled down over her shoulders, hiding her face, but he heard her reply. "Yes, I'll wait."

She relaxed in his arms now, and Johnny told his love. "I thought of you these six years, every single moment. At night I dreamed of you. You kept me from tragedy, Polly, when nothing else worked. Two years seems longer than eternity, now, but God didn't bring us together to separate us. Only for two years. Do you see the hand of God in this?"

She nodded wordlessly. "Polly," he went on, "such a promise as you just gave me—should be sealed with a kiss." He brushed back the fine strands of curls and tilted up her chin with one finger. "Polly, please?" Since she didn't move, he kissed her cheek. "Polly? You must kiss back to seal the promise."

Suddenly she looked him full in the face, her eyes exploring his. He kissed her on the mouth. She was sweeter than honeysuckle. Once, only. He kept his promise.

Lines from an old love poem ran through his head, but because it was too soon, he only thought the words as he looked at her.

> *Around the world, dear heart, I longed for thee;*
> *And calm and storm, your name gave hope to me.*
> *And now I rest, in harbor stilled,*
> *My cup of love is filled.*

Epilogue

On February 12, 1750, John Newton married Mary (Polly) Catlett at Chatham, England. He was twenty-five years old, and she was twenty-two. Three sea voyages followed, where he commanded a ship. In 1754, due to ill health, John retired from sea life and became surveyor of the tides at Liverpool.

In 1760 he became pastor of a small, independent church at Warwick. In 1764 he was an ordained minister with a church at Olney. That year he published a story of his life at sea. John Newton wrote a total of 280 hymns, the most well-known being: "Amazing Grace," "How Sweet the Name of Jesus Sounds," and "Glorious Things of Thee Are Spoken."

John Newton's voyages were involved with the slave trade, but he often said he was shocked at a job always connected with chains, bolts, and shackles. He hated to think of himself as a jailor. He prayed that the Lord would place him in a more humane calling. The rigid class system of England at that time blinded the eyes of people to the Bible teaching of equality.

The common people were not encouraged to read the Bible for themselves. The verse in Exodus 21:16 seemed to be unknown: "And he that stealeth a man and selleth him, or if he be found in his hand, he shall surely be put to death." Life at sea and life ashore was harsh, and men were glad to take any job they could find.

From Olney, John Newton moved to London and was pastor of a church there. He began to speak out more openly against the slave trade. In 1763, he wrote a statement: "It was a cross which I bore with patience until He delivered me from it. I treated the slaves under my care with gentleness and took care for their comfort."

In 1788, John Newton published a paper telling of his experience in the slave trade. By 1791 he grew bolder as his conscience and the conscience of the nation were awakened regarding its evils. He wrote: "My conscience and guilt force me to speak out. The true conditions of the slave trade have been brought to light. It is a national sin of crimson dye."

His writings were published widely, and he received letters from all parts of the world, agreeing with him and praising him for the stand he took against slavery.

The University of New Jersey offered him an honorary Doctor of Divinity degree, but Newton refused it, feeling himself not worthy.

Newton witnessed before Parliament about the evils of slavery and told his own experiences. Because he had been a slave, he could speak from experience. He said: "My confession comes too late to repair some of the mischief I took part in. I admit I was active in a business at which my heart now shudders. There was never any excuse for the slave trade."

In a sermon in 1794, he said: "There is a cry of blood against us—a cry from hundreds of thousands sold into slavery."

In 1797 he preached: "The blood of many thousands of helpless fellowmen is crying against us. Slaves are torn from families, homes, and native lands. Enough of this horrid scene. The African slave trade is a national sin."

In 1804, when he was seventy-nine years old, Newton told a friend: "For forty years I have thought every waking hour of my former misery [in the slave trade]."

Newton returned one year, as captain of a ship, to the Plantane Islands and actually picked the limes from trees he had planted as a slave. He sent a boat and invited Kiringa aboard and served her a feast. At first she was terrified, but Newton loaded her with presents and sent her home in peace.

Polly Newton died December, 1790, of cancer. John Newton died December, 1807, the year that brought the end of the slave trade among all Englishmen. The Bill for Abolition stated that all manner of dealing and trading of slaves was unlawful and a crime. In the thirty years before this law, about 120,000 slaves a year crossed the Atlantic in slave ships.

Newton chose these words for his tombstone: "John Newton, clerk, once an unbeliever and great sinner, a servant of slaves the old African blasphemer."

If John Newton had left nothing else to the world besides his best-known hymn, his life still has blessed millions of people through the song "Amazing Grace."

> Amazing grace—how sweet the sound—
> That saved a wretch like me!
> I once was lost but now am found,
> Was blind but now I see.
>
> 'Twas grace that taught my heart to fear,
> And grace my fears relieved;
> How precious did that grace appear
> The hour I first believed!
>
> Thru many dangers, toils and snares
> I have already come;
> 'Tis grace hath brought me safe thus far,
> And grace will lead me home.
>
> The earth shall soon dissolve like snow;
> The sun forbear to shine;
> But God, Who called me here below,
> Will be forever mine.

When we've been there ten thousand years
Bright shining as the sun,
We've no less days to sing God's praise
Than when we'd first begun.

JOHN NEWTON

Glossary

ballast—Any heavy substance used in a boat to control its stability.

belaying pin—A peg around which a rope is twisted to hold it secure.

bosun—Short for *boatswain,* an officer in charge of rigging, anchors, and cable.

bulwark—The side of a ship above the upper deck; a railing.

burgoo—A thick oatmeal porridge.

Canton White—A flag in which one-quarter of the upper corner contains the national emblem.

capstan—A revolving cylinder that winds up rope which is pulling a weight.

chain shot—Two small cannon balls attached by a chain, used in a cannon.

chippy—A street girl.

cracker hash—A thin, hard biscuit chopped up with water or gravy.

crosstrees—Two horizontal pieces of timber at the head of a lower mast.

crow's nest—A platform, or lookout, up high on a mast.

dandy funk—Thin, hard biscuit soaked in water and cooked with molasses and grease.

dogwatch—The hours from 4:00 to 6:00 P.M. and from 6:00 to 8:00 P.M.

Doldrums—A section of the sea near the equator, with weak winds or none.

Ensign Red—A flag of a merchant ship in the 1700s in England.

forecastle (fo'c'sle)—The forward part of the vessel, where sailors sleep.

foremast—The mast nearest the bow, or front of the ship.

galley—The kitchen of a sailing ship.

grapeshot—A cluster of small, iron balls used as cannon shot.

grog—Watery liquor.

gunwale—Where topsides and deck meet and guns are mounted.

the Horn—The southern tip of South America, a dangerous spot for ships, due to the weather.

jolly boat—A small boat carried on a ship; lifeboat.

keel—The timbers that extend along the center of the ship's bottom.

keelhauled—Attaching a man to a rope and dragging him under the keel of the ship as punishment.

leeward—Opposite of windward; the side of the ship away from the weather.

lifeline—An anchored rope across the ship's deck, used to cling to in storms.

longboat—The largest boat carried by a merchant ship.

mainsail—The most important sail on the mainmast.

man-of-war—A war vessel armed for defense and attack.

midshipman—A sailor who is learning on the job to become an officer.

mizzenmast—The aftermost mast, toward the stern of a ship.

mutiny—A riot or uprising, refusal to obey orders on a ship.

port (direction)—The left side of a ship, looking from stern to bow.

press-gang—A group of the king's navy men who kidnapped people and forced them to work on a ship.

purser—Clerk who keeps the accounts.

ratlines—Small, transverse ropes attached to the shrouds and forming a rope ladder.

rigging—The ropes and chains that raise and lower the masts and spars.

Rutter—A handbook of information for sailors in the 1700s.

salt junk—Hard salted beef.

scurvy—A disease causing spongy, bleeding gums, resulting from lack of Vitamin C.

sea chest—A wooden locker in which a sailor kept his belongings.

sextant—An instrument used at sea for measuring longitudes and latitudes.

ship biscuit—Hard, dry biscuits.

sick berth—A section of a ship used as hospital.

slumgullion—A sloppy soup made of leftovers.

Spanish Main—The mainland of South America.

starboard—Opposite of port; the right side of the ship as one faces the bow.

main topgallant sail—A sail on the middle mast, fourth from the bottom.

topsail—One of the sails on the middle (main) mast.

trade winds—A wind blowing from the east toward the equator.

trick—A shift, a period of duty.

watch—A period of duty four hours long.

windward—In the direction of the wind; opposite of leeward, islands of the West Indies.

yardarm—Either end of a long spar which supports a sail.

CHRISTIAN HERALD ASSOCIATION AND ITS MINISTRIES

CHRISTIAN HERALD ASSOCIATION, founded in 1878, publishes The Christian Herald Magazine, one of the leading interdenominational religious monthlies in America. Through its wide circulation, it brings inspiring articles and the latest news of religious developments to many families. From the magazine's pages came the initiative for CHRISTIAN HERALD CHILDREN and THE BOWERY MISSION, two individually supported not-for-profit corporations.

CHRISTIAN HERALD CHILDREN, established in 1894, is the name for a unique and dynamic ministry to disadvantaged children, offering hope and opportunities which would not otherwise be available for reasons of poverty and neglect. The goal is to develop each child's potential and to demonstrate Christian compassion and understanding to children in need.

Mont Lawn is a permanent camp located in Bushkill, Pennsylvania. It is the focal point of a ministry which provides a healthful "vacation with a purpose" to children who without it would be confined to the streets of the city. Up to 1000 children between the age of 7 and 11 come to Mont Lawn each year.

Christian Herald Children maintains year-round contact with children by means of a *City Youth Ministry.* Central to its philosophy is the belief that only through sustained relationships and demonstrated concern can individual lives be truly enriched. Special emphasis is on individual guidance, spiritual and family counseling and tutoring. This follow-up ministry to inner-city children culminates for many in financial assistance toward higher education and career counseling.

THE BOWERY MISSION, located at 227 Bowery, New York City, has since 1879 been reaching out to the lost men on the Bowery, offering them what could be their last chance to rebuild their lives. Every man is fed, clothed and ministered to. Countless numbers have entered the 90-day residential rehabilitation program at the Bowery Mission. A concentrated ministry of counseling, medical care, nutrition therapy, Bible study and Gospel services awakens a man to spiritual renewal within himself.

These ministries are supported solely by the voluntary contributions of individuals and by legacies and bequests. Contributions are tax deductible. Checks should be made out either to CHRISTIAN HERALD CHILDREN or to THE BOWERY MISSION.

Administrative Office: 40 Overlook Drive, Chappaqua, New York 10514
Telephone: (914) 769-9000